AMERICAN HERITAGE

August 1962 · Volume XIII, Number 5

All the ebullient imagination of childhood suddenly released from school-room routine is in The Old Stage Coach, *painted in 1871 by the Maine artist Eastman Johnson. With a "Gee up!" the driver puts a whip to his faithful steeds, and a passenger bolder than the rest waves farewell from the lurching roof. Two ladies, late as usual, scurry to board before departure. The driver will wait: they're bringing the lunch.*

AMERICAN HERITAGE

The Magazine of History

PUBLISHER
James Parton

EDITORIAL DIRECTOR
Joseph J. Thorndike, Jr.

SENIOR EDITOR
Bruce Catton

EDITOR
Oliver Jensen

ASSOCIATE EDITORS
Robert Cowley
E. M. Halliday
Richard M. Ketchum
Joan Paterson Mills
Robert L. Reynolds

ASSISTANT EDITORS
Meryle Evans, Stephen W. Sears

CONTRIBUTING EDITOR
Margery Darrell

LIBRARIAN
Caroline Backlund

COPY EDITOR
Beverly Hill
ASSISTANT: Suzanne Smith

SENIOR ART DIRECTOR
Irwin Glusker

ART DIRECTOR
Murray Belsky
STAFF PHOTOGRAPHER: Herbert Loebel

ADVISORY BOARD
Allan Nevins, *Chairman*

Carl Carmer   Alvin M. Josephy, Jr.
Albert B. Corey   Richard P. McCormick
Christopher Crittenden   Harry Shaw Newman
Marshall B. Davidson   Howard H. Peckham
Louis C. Jones   S. K. Stevens
Arthur M. Schlesinger, Sr.

AMERICAN HERITAGE is published every two months by American Heritage Publishing Co., Inc., 551 Fifth Avenue, New York 17, N.Y. Correspondence about subscriptions should be addressed to: American Heritage Subscription Office, 383 West Center Street, Marion, Ohio. Single Copies: $3.95. Annual Subscriptions: $15.00 in U.S. & Canada; $16.00 elsewhere.

An annual Index of AMERICAN HERITAGE is published every February, priced at $1.00. A Cumulative Index of Volumes VI–X is available at $3.00.

AMERICAN HERITAGE will consider but assumes no responsibility for unsolicited material.
Title registered U.S. Patent Office.
Second class postage paid at New York, N.Y.

Sponsored by

American Association for State & Local History · Society of American Historians

CONTENTS   *August 1962 · Volume XIII, Number 5*

COVER: A detail from John Trumbull's highly romanticized *The Battle of Bunker Hill—June 17, 1775,* painted a decade later in Benjamin West's London studio, and now at the Yale University Art Gallery. The central figure is the dying Major General Joseph Warren of Massachusetts, "the greatest incendiary in all America." Other colonists identified in the miniature key at right are: General Israel Putnam (2) of Connecticut; Colonel William Prescott (3) of Massachusetts, who had fortified Breed's Hill; Lieutenant Colonel John Parker (4), the hero of Lexington; Captain Thomas Knowlton (5) of Connecticut; Major Andrew McClary (6) of New Hampshire; Major Willard Moore (7) of Massachusetts; and a clergyman identified by Trumbull only as "Reverᵈ Mʳ McClintock" (8). British officers include the senior commanders, Generals William Howe (9) and Henry Clinton (10), and Major John Small (11). An excerpt from Richard M. Ketchum's *The Battle for Bunker Hill* begins on page 80. *Back Cover:* Trade cards from the Warshaw Collection of Business Americana.

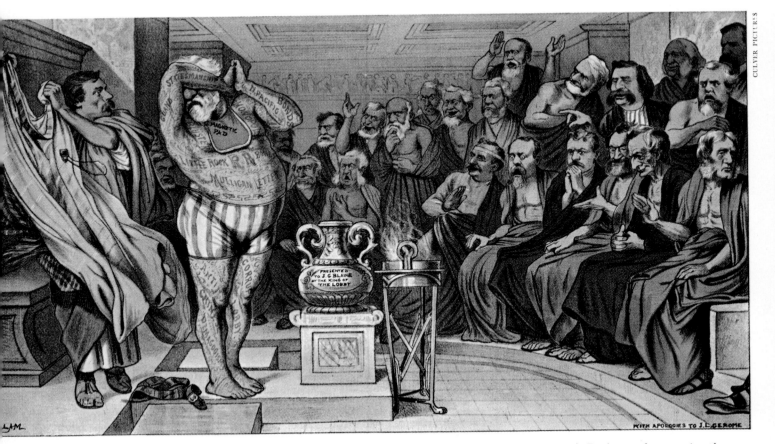

Phryne Before the Chicago Tribunal. *Bernhard Gillam's caustic drawing in the Democratic* Puck, *set the tone for the campaign. A parody of a then-popular French painting of Phryne, lovely Greek courtesan, being unveiled to the gaze of Athenian statesmen, it shows James G. Blaine in a comparable situation before leaders of the Republican party. His various special-interest deals show up as ugly tattoos, and even his renowned personal magnetism is represented as a cheap fraud.*

The first volleys in America's "vilest" presidential campaign were fired on July 21, 1884, when a small Buffalo paper exposed a shocking personal scandal involving the Democratic candidate, Grover Cleveland, then governor of New York. Cleveland, big, slow-moving, forthright, "foursquare," had become a popular image of decency and public honesty; he had been elected on a reform ticket by a 200,000 majority over an entrenched Republican machine, and he was expected to cleanse New York of corruption. It now appeared that in 1874 he had seduced a widow, one Maria Halpin, fathered her child, and refused to marry her. Cleveland did not deny this adventure. When friends asked him how to reply to the scandal, he said, "Tell the truth."

Rumors grew and spread: that the Governor was a habitual drunkard and libertine; that in Albany he kept "women" convenient to the executive mansion; that he was being secretly treated for a "malignant" disease. . . . Reminders of his bastard boy were chanted through the streets in great Republican parades:

> *Ma! Ma! Where's my Pa?*
> *Gone to the White House—Ha! Ha! Ha!*

The nation was shocked. The president of Amherst declared that only voters of debauched moral sentiment could support Cleveland. Ministers throughout the country preached sermons on his sins. The Reverend George Ball of Buffalo proclaimed:

The issue is evidently not between the two great parties, but between the brothel and the family, between indecency and decency, between lust and law, between the essence of barbarism and the first principles of civilization, between the degradation of woman and due honor, protection, and love to our mothers, sisters and daughters.

THE DIRTIEST ELECTION

By MARVIN AND
DOROTHY ROSENBERG

Frank Beard's cartoon in Judge, *a Republican weekly, was far from subtle about Grover Cleveland's offense. Captioned* Another Voice for Cleveland, *it left little room for doubt as to the paternity of the bawling infant. In actuality, the evidence was not that clear.*

This set the tone of the campaign. Would Victorian America elect an unchaste, "immoral" man President? The answer, after months of vicious "moral" warfare, would turn on such unrelated events as the collapse of an ex-President's business, the support of Cleveland by a famous Protestant minister who had himself been charged with adultery, and the last-minute emergence of the "Catholic problem." But most of all, it would depend on the strange character of Cleveland's brilliant Republican opponent, James G. Blaine, one of America's master politicians.

Elegant and polished, passionately ambitious, Blaine was a dangerous complex of strengths and weaknesses, of intellectual perception and moral obtuseness. He grasped power easily, but he used it mainly for power's sake. He was a superb congressional tactician, first as Speaker of the House, then as senator; he was known

as "magnetic" the country over for his power to charm and persuade; but he was also called "Slippery Jim" because the most conspicuous end of his subtle manipulation of men and laws had been to protect himself and his party from investigations by the Democrats.

There was much to defend. Authority came too easily to the Republicans after the Civil War. With the Democrats disorganized and disgraced as the "party of treason," their southern strongholds in the hands of carpetbaggers, the Republicans' power was enormous, and they were enormously corrupted. There has been more spectacular malfeasance in Washington, but nothing to match the persistent, hungry stealing that honeycombed Grant's administration.

The great Panic of 1873 laid bare the corruption, and the angry Democrats roared back to win the House. Blaine found himself in the middle of Re-

However spurious, the celebrated characterization of Blaine as a "plumed knight" was in keeping with this noble pose.

publican civil war. Grant's henchmen, the Stalwarts, led by the formidable Senator Roscoe Conkling of New York, frankly held to the spoils system as a means of retaining the party's power, and bitterly attacked the "rancid, canting self-righteousness" of a rising band of reform-minded Independent Republicans, called—at first scornfully and then popularly—the Mugwumps, who set out to rescue their party and nation from the spoilsmen. Blaine moved restlessly between the Stalwarts and the Independents, identifying himself with neither but choosing a third faction—more responsible than the Stalwarts, more "practical" than the Mugwumps—who were known as the Half-Breeds.

To the Mugwumps, Slippery Jim Blaine was stained with collusion, graft, and perjury. He wanted money too much; he had grown rich too quickly, rich far beyond the potentials of his congressional salary. For financial favors, he had twisted laws and tricked colleagues; he had acted as a salesman of railway securities while, as Speaker of the House, he tenderly shepherded legislation to help the burgeoning new railroads. Most notorious was his involvement with the Little Rock and Fort Smith Railroad. He had

made a ruling which enriched this line, and for his efforts he had been given considerable holdings in it.

Something of this leaked out in the spring of 1876, from letters written by Blaine to a railroad executive named Warren Fisher and preserved by James Mulligan, who was Fisher's bookkeeper. In one of the most damaging of these "Mulligan letters," Blaine enclosed an alibi for himself, which he wanted Fisher to copy, sign, and return: Blaine endorsed the missive, *Burn this letter*. Fisher did not burn it, and a rhythmic street chant that would haunt Blaine throughout the 1884 campaign was, *"Burn this letter! Burn this letter! Burn, burn, oh burn this letter!"*

But in 1876, that letter had not yet been exposed, and "Magnetic Jim's" daring method of smothering many of the others remains one of the great tours de force in the history of Congress. A Democratic-controlled Judiciary Committee was prying into Blaine's affairs; Mulligan was summoned to bring his letters to Washington to testify. The Republican convention was only a few days off, and Blaine, the favorite Half-Breed candidate, needed a clean slate to enter it. The nation was watching. Blaine went privately to see Mulligan, who refused to give up the letters: he would need them in case his own veracity were questioned. Then, Mulligan said later, Blaine hinted at the gift of a political office, and when this failed, he knelt and begged for the correspondence as a mercy to his wife and children; he even threatened suicide. Well, said Mulligan, Blaine could *look* at the letters. Blaine then seized what Mulligan showed him, and departed.

When the time was ripe, Blaine rose in the House on a point of privilege, and with virtuous indignation held aloft the packet of letters, which he would not let the committee have. Why should he, he asked. Would any gentleman be "willing and ready to have his private correspondence scanned over and be made public?" No! But, Blaine added emotionally,

I am not afraid to show them. Thank God Almighty, I am not afraid to show them . . . There is the very original package. And with some sense of humiliation, with a mortification that I do not pretend to conceal, with a sense of outrage which I think any man in my position would feel, I invite the confidence of the forty-four million of my countrymen while I read those letters . . .

From the Republicans, there was wild applause. Blaine went on with his amazing performance. He read the letters out of order, adding his own comment and interpretation to confuse their implications. What of Mulligan's testimony? Nonsense all, he said. There had been no threat of suicide, no begging. Well, he might have made a "joking reference" to a political office for the man . . . It was a magnificent, magnetic show, and rapt Republican spectators exonerated him.

At the Republican convention in 1876, Blaine was one of the favorites. Colonel Robert Ingersoll, that grandiloquent orator, placed his name in nomination with an allusion to his great self-defense in the House, and conferred on him an enduring image: "Like an armed warrior, like a *plumed knight,* James G. Blaine marched down the halls of the American Congress and threw his shining lance full and fair against the brazen foreheads of the defamers of his country and the maligners of his honor . . ."

But the Mugwumps were not persuaded. To them, as to the Democrats, Blaine stood convicted of "trading upon his high official position for his own advantage," and he lost the nomination to the impeccable Rutherford B. Hayes.

Now, in 1884, Blaine had finally won his party's endorsement to run against Cleveland. The voters faced a hard choice: between a state governor who had dallied with a widow and refused to marry her when she became a mother, and a profiteering congressman who had taken "gifts" from business and lied about them, who had urged laws to favor his partners and line his pockets. The choice, as a Mugwump newspaper asserted, was between a private immoralist and a public immoralist.

In the fierce campaign, the usual political issues took second place. The violent passions between the agricultural, free-trade Democrats and the industrial, protectionist Republicans were receding, and the war wounds were healing. But the nation was emotional over the matter of sin; citizens turned out excitedly for mass street parades, and argued heatedly about good and evil.

Both candidates were harassed not only by the vicious attacks of their enemies, but also by the spectacular bumbling of friends trying to help. Cleveland got the worst of it, because the thrusts at him were so personal, so irrelevant to his public record. Politically, he was known as "bone honest," even "ugly honest," for his relentless war on civic graft and grafters. To some Democrats, his appointments seemed fair to the point of extravagance. General Edward S. Bragg, in nominating him, said "men loved him for the enemies he made." The very invulnerability of his public record seemed to intensify the indignation of the moralists at his private peccadillo. As they raked over his sins, they made the months between July and November an agony Cleveland never forgot.

The Reverend Mr. Ball of Buffalo, who claimed to speak for a ministerial investigating committee, asserted that the New York governor had "accomplished the seduction" of Mrs. Halpin, the director of the

"Foursquare," a popular epithet for Cleveland, had a physical as well as moral basis: he weighed more than 250 pounds.

cloak and lace department of a Buffalo store. The report went on to say,

that the woman, so far as known, had borne an irreproachable character up to that time; that her employers, with whom she had been about four years, had a high regard for her and considered her a virtuous Christian woman; that Mr. Cleveland had taken her to the Lying-in Hospital during her confinement; that the woman became depressed and threatened his life; that he became apprehensive that she might attempt some injury to him or herself and appealed to the Chief of Police, Colonel John Byrne, to keep her under surveillance; that Mr. Cleveland had her taken by force from her room at Mrs. Baker's to the Providence Lunatic Asylum . . . that she was seen there by Doctor Ring, who did not think her insane; that after several days she escaped and no efforts were made to retake her; that she put her case into the hands of Milo A. Whitney, Esq., an attorney, alleging kidnapping and false imprisonment; that she finally gave up the child and received $500 from Mr. Cleveland . . . that these are matters of common repute in Buffalo, to substantiate which numerous witnesses can be found . . .

Worse than the specific charges were the spreading innuendos that the Halpin affair was not a momentary aberration. The Reverend Mr. Ball contributed to them with lurid accusations:

Investigations disclose still more proof of debaucheries too horrible to relate and too vile to be readily believed. For many years days devoted to business have been followed by nights of sin. He has lived a bachelor; had no home, *avoiding the restraints even of hotel or boarding house life,* lodged in rooms on the third floor in a business block, and made those rooms a harem; foraged outside, also, in the city and surrounding villages; a champion libertine, an artful seducer, a foe to virtue, an enemy of the family, a snare to youth and hostile to true womanhood. The Halpin case was not solitary. Women now married and anxious to cover the sins of their youth have been his victims, and are now alarmed lest their relations with him shall be exposed. Some disgraced and broken-hearted victims of his lust now slumber in the grave. Since he has become governor of this great state he has not abated his lecheries. Abundant rumors implicate him at Albany, and well-authenticated facts convict him at Buffalo.

Ball's attacks could be read in full in such proper newspapers as Lucy Stone's suffragette *Woman's Journal,* which viewed the nomination of Cleveland as a kind of personal affront to all decent women. In a remarkable piece of fairness, however, her *Journal* published the opposite view of a Mugwump correspondent, Colonel T. Wentworth Higginson, who, though firmly against sin, delicately proposed that unbroken integrity was more important than unbroken chastity. But the editors and their other correspondents insisted repeatedly that sexual sin was a sign of total moral decay.

In the letters and editorials there is often on one hand scorn for a male seducer, and on the other, feminist anger that he might be getting away with a sin prohibited to women. But the manifest argument was always for defense of family and home, women's special care. Lucy spoke of a solemn fear that was echoed throughout the nation—the lamentable effect of Cleveland's example on America's young men. His candidacy "fills half the newspapers in the United States with apologies for a degrading vice—apologies which every profligate man and fast youth will appropriate to his own justification."

The worst rumors about Cleveland were unpublishable, even in the most sensational papers, but they spread by pamphlet and whisper: the "whores" in Albany, the "malignant" disease. Some, the *Nation* complained, were "so improbable and so filthy that they seem to have been hatched by street-walkers and sold to Dr. Ball for a dollar apiece." Many ministers began to assure their congregations that Cleveland was excluded from all decent houses; even the Reverend Henry Ward Beecher, to Cleveland's dismay, was said to be on the verge of turning against him.

Cleveland's inauguration on March 4, 1885, drew a wildly enthusiastic crowd, estimated at 40,000, to the east front of the

A Mugwump and potential friend, Beecher was uniquely desirable as a supporter, for this great spiritual leader had been through a sensational trial as an adulterer and had still kept the respect of a substantial part of the nation. Cleveland wrote in anguish to Mrs. Beecher that "the contemptible creatures who coin and pass these things appear to think that the affair which I have not denied makes me defenseless against any and all slanders." There was more he could say, but he wanted to say it to Beecher himself. "Cannot I manage to see him and tell him what I cannot write?" Whatever Cleveland's unwritable excuses were, Beecher, who had been considering the matter for a long time, made his decision. He came out for the "immoral" Governor, and vigorously attacked Blaine's "a-whoring after votes."

Unfortunately for Cleveland, the support of Beecher and other well-intentioned friends did him more harm than good. Some friendly Mugwumps only gave wider notice to the rumors by loudly denying that Cleveland was a libertine and a drunkard, or that he had "recently taken part in a drunken debauch in Buffalo." The Reverend Kinsley Twining, while speaking for those clergymen who supported the Governor, only managed to make his sins specific. Twining had investigated the scandals, and conceded that when Cleveland was younger

Capitol. Their hero, surviving charges of personal vice, had led the Democrats to victory for the first time since the Civil War.

he was guilty of an illicit connection; but . . . there was no seduction, no adultery, no breach of promise, no obligation of marriage; but there was a culpable irregularity of life, living as he was, a bachelor, for which it was proper and is proper that he should suffer. After the primary offense, which is not to be palliated in the circle for which I write, his conduct was singularly honorable.

There was a bad sound to this, whatever Cleveland's formal responsibilities; and though Twining went on to refute the spreading charges of "general libertinism and drunkenness," though he called Cleveland "a man of true and kind heart, frank and open" and assured Independent Republicans that Cleveland's error was not such as to "placate them toward Blaine," still he was not easy about the Halpin affair: "It is a fact in the history of their candidate which they cannot forget and which they will have to carry as a burden."

Beecher, for his part, did Cleveland no good by declaring that he only atoned for a sin that many men shared. Beecher's flamboyant declaration—that if every New Yorker who had broken the Seventh Commandment voted for Cleveland, he would be elected by a 200,000 majority—was described by the Republican New York *Tribune* as a call to adulterers to vote Democratic. To be the victim of such support could hardly have been comforting to Cleveland. But the friends who troubled him most were those who tried to find

other fathers for the bastard boy. The New York *World* quoted one such defense:

While Cleveland was "sowing his wildoats," he met this woman . . . and became intimate with her. She was a widow, and not a good woman by any means. Mr. Cleveland, learning this, began to make inquiries about her, and discovered that two of his friends were intimate with her at the same time as himself. When a child was born, Cleveland, in order to shield his two friends, who were both married men, assumed the responsibility of it.

An outraged writer to the *Woman's Journal* retorted that "If such was the real character of the woman" then Cleveland's act showed him to be a "low dirty fellow."

The Governor's best defenders were those hardheaded friends who simply conceded his past and argued that it was unimportant compared with Blaine's dishonesty in office. The *Nation* said frankly that his "sin" would disqualify him "if his opponent be free from this stain, and as good a man in all other ways." But the sins of Blaine, the magazine claimed, were intolerable in a statesman, while, in philandering, Cleveland had only followed in the footsteps of other great and lusty politicians. A witty Mugwump summed up this philosophy: "We should elect Mr. Cleveland to the public office he is so admirably qualified to fill and remand Mr. Blaine to the private life he is so eminently fitted to adorn."

But an irony developed here. While no grounds were found for seriously accusing Cleveland of dishonesty, a strange story about Blaine's private life turned up, and was offered to Cleveland as campaign fodder. Though Blaine had himself been instrumental in spreading the Buffalo scandal, Cleveland had shunned retaliation on a personal level. To the surprise of his secretary, Daniel Lamont, and his friend William Hudson, the Governor asked to talk to the talebearer of the Blaine gossip. As Hudson told it, Cleveland took the man's documentary proofs, paid him "for his expenses, the time he . . . lost, and his good will in the matter," and sent him away. Next, Cleveland put the documents on his desk, and brought out others he had received earlier.

Then, drawing a waste basket to him, the Governor began to tear them into small bits, to the unbounded astonishment of Lamont and myself. When he had finished that lot he took up the proofs brought that morning and destroyed them in the same manner. No words were spoken by anyone until the Governor called a porter and directed him to burn in the fireplace the scraps of paper, standing over him to watch the process. When all were consumed he came back to where Lamont and I were standing, and said to Lamont: "The other side can have a monopoly of all the dirt in this campaign."

CONTINUED ON PAGE 97

9

As the ever-observant Gibbon noted long ago, mankind is much more liberal with applause for its destroyers than for its benefactors. What other explanation can there be for the fact that nowhere, despite thousands of parks and squares bristling with military statuary, has his adopted country erected a statue to John Matthews? A benefactor of the first rank, Matthews gave us the soda fountain and popularized carbonated drinks, yet his only personal memorial is his grave in Greenwood Cemetery, Brooklyn. It is, to be sure, no mean monument, for above a recumbent marble likeness of Matthews rises a granite Gothic canopy and spire to a height of thirty-six feet, richly carved all over with gargoyles, evangelists, expiring Matthews relatives, flora, fauna, and elaborate bas-reliefs representing great moments in the life of the deceased. De-

signed and partially executed in his own workshop, this imposing potpourri looks very much like one of Matthews' own "cottage" soda fountains at the height of that eclectic art form. But the benefactor's true monument is to be found in nearly every drugstore, luncheonette, and department store in America; his handiwork lives on every Main Street.

Natural carbonated waters have, of course, been bubbling up out of springs and spas since the dawn of history. Paracelsus, Lavoisier, and Dr. Joseph Priestley observed and experimented with them. A Swedish chemist named Bergman produced artificial carbonated or mineral water in 1770, and Professor Benjamin Silliman of Yale began manufacturing and bottling small quantities in New Haven in 1806. An early fountain was dispensing various homemade Vichy, Kissingen, and Apollinaris "seltzers" in New

THE SODA Fountain

Of bubbling waters, sacred marble, and old John Matthews, father of an industry and a flamboyant art form

By JOSEPH L. MORRISON

York by 1810; they were supposed to cure obesity. But it was the arrival of John Matthews in New York about 1832 that made soda-water drinking an industry and, incidentally, offered the grogshop and the saloon the first real competition they had ever encountered.

As students of the Matthews mausoleum can learn by twisting their necks to observe the canopy's carved ceiling, the benefactor-to-be began as an apprentice in the London shop of Joseph Bramah, inventor, among other things, of the permutation bank lock, a hydraulic press, and a new kind of seamless lead tubing. There, in eternal stone, is young John, learning how to construct machinery to make carbonic acid gas. In an adjoining panel, he appears again, aged twenty-one, taking ship to seek his fortune in New York, doubtless convinced that there was no future for a seltzer man in a nation of confirmed tea-drinkers.

Matthews hung out his shingle at 55 Gold Street and was soon manufacturing carbonating machinery and selling charged water to retail stores. The equipment was simple enough—a cast-iron box, lined with lead, where carbonic acid gas was formed by the action of sulphuric acid (then often called oil of vitriol) on marble dust. The gas was then purified by passing it through water, and conducted into a tank partially filled with cool water. An employee rocked the tank for a quarter to a half hour, until the water was impregnated and bubbly. To imitate popular mineral waters, one added their salts to the mixture.

The introduction of marble chips was an American development, for Bramah had used whiting and chalk. But marble was easier and cheaper to come by in New York: the enterprising Matthews firm at one point acquired all the scrap from the building of St. Patrick's Cathedral in New York. Although a few of the devout thought this use unseemly, these chips alone supplied some twenty-five million gallons before the supply gave out. Pressure, of course, is always a hazard in gas manufacture, and there were a number of noisy explosions among Matthews' competitors in the early days, but his firm had a special, if rather unusual, method of keeping the pressure from rising above the optimum level of 150 pounds.

The safety valve was an ex-slave named Ben Austen, one of the earliest employees, a man of intelligence and, above all, strength. When the force of a new batch of soda water needed measuring, the job fell to Ben, who simply placed his powerful thumb over the pressure cock. When it blew his thumb away, the Matthews people estimated they had reached 150 pounds and that the water was fully charged. "Ben's Thumb" was long a term in the jargon of the trade. During the Civil War draft riots, when angry Irish mobs roamed the New York streets seeking to hang any Negro they could find, Matthews was obliged to ship Ben out to safety in a packing case, as though he were a tank of the product.

As time went on, several strong competitors entered the field—John Lippincott of Philadelphia, A. D. Puffer of Boston, and James W. Tufts of Somerville, Massachusetts (he did so well eventually that he founded Pinehurst, North Carolina)—but the next great breakthrough, and the one which brought them all prosperity, was made in 1838 or 1839 by Eugene Roussel, a Frenchman who was selling plain soda water at his perfume shop in Philadelphia. With the ingenuity that characterizes all Frenchmen when dealing with the opposite sex, he decided to add flavors to his customers' drinks. As simple as that, but no one had thought of it. Soon the crude soda fountains of Matthews and his competitors were all keeping syrups on hand, in orange, cherry, lemon, teaberry, ginger, peach, and many other flavors. Root beer and birch beer and sarsaparilla appeared, bottled or made at the fountain. Attempts were made to imitate, without alcohol, the flavors of various wines and champagnes, but apparently less successfully.

For a very modest investment, Matthews could put any chemist or other entrepreneur in business. Here is one offering:

1 upright generator	$115.00
1 four-gallon fountain frame	25.00
1 draught apparatus for counter	40.00
6 patent soda tumblers	1.25
1 case extracts for syrups	6.00
1 barrel Matthews' ground marble (Ah, there, St. Patrick!)	2.00
165 lbs. sulphuric acid with carboy	6.53
	195.78

Only six tumblers were provided, but they could be washed in a jiffy. They were simply rinsed in cold water, for germs concerned nobody, and their existence was not suspected. Ice cooling had been introduced and business was booming, so that Art, which had been waiting in the wings, could now step forward and embrace Commerce. The Leonardo of the soda fountain was one G. D. Dows, of Lowell, Massachusetts, who decided to try his hand at improving the looks of the crude soda fountain in his brother's store, and wound up with a combination fountain and ice shaver housed in a white Italian marble box. It became so popular that Dows opened his own place in Boston.

The "cottage" fountain, as this kind of design was later called, now took over the field. Basically boxes resting on a counter, they ran riot through the art of decoration—Gothic, Roman, Byzantine, Egyptian, Japanese, Brooklyn Hittite, anything in any combination—

11

and bore names like The Frost King, The Icefloe, The Egyptian, The Avalanche, and The Cathedral. Fanciful spigots led out of tombs and temples and chalets decorated with sphinxes, lions, nymphs, knights; allegory ran wild. Names of flavors and famous mineral waters would appear on the larger models. There is a tale of an old lady who walked around a giant fountain displayed at a fete in the Seventh Regiment Armory in New York, reading off to herself the distinguished names graven next to each spigot: Saratoga, Deep Rock, Kissingen, Washington. Then she turned to the attendant. "I didn't know," she said, "that the gallant Seventh had fought in all these battles."

In 1870, John Matthews was gathered to his fathers and entombed in the elegant manner we have described. Meanwhile the "cottage" became too small a device, what with the hundreds of flavors now offered, and great wall-models now appeared, erected like altars behind the counter, gleaming in marble and onyx and with even more fanciful architecture. One boasted 300 flavors. Another cost $40,000, a fortune in those days.

Now another great benefactor appeared, who united the ice cream parlor and the soda fountain. Although he has rival claimants, the historians of the industry press the accolade for inventing the ice cream soda upon Robert M. Green, the soft-drink concessionaire at the Franklin Institute Exposition held in Philadelphia in 1874. Among the drinks he had been selling was one concocted of fresh sweet cream, syrup, and carbonated water, but one busy day he ran out of cream. In desperation he bought some vanilla ice cream, intending to melt it, but the customers were so pressing that he used it in its congealed form. Apparently the drinkers uttered glad cries of joy, for Green thereafter made ice cream sodas *on purpose,* and the recipe spread over the country.

By the end of the century, the soda fountain was big business. The four original firms had combined, as was then stylish, into a trust. It was no longer necessary for soda-fountain proprietors to make their own gas, behind the counter or in the cellar, because it could now be purchased in portable steel cylinders. The wall temples began to disappear in favor of the modern counter, with the apparatus hidden inside it, and the great empty space where the old fountain had stood was covered with an ornate looking-glass and clever displays of tumblers—washed nowadays in hot water. Food too was now offered for sale, and in the twenties came mechanical refrigeration. It was a long way from Lavoisier, from the dissenting parson Priestley shaking up the first glass of artificial mineral water with gas acquired at a nearby brewery, from Ben's thumb, and from that great silent soda fountain in Greenwood Cemetery. But a great thirst had at last been quenched.

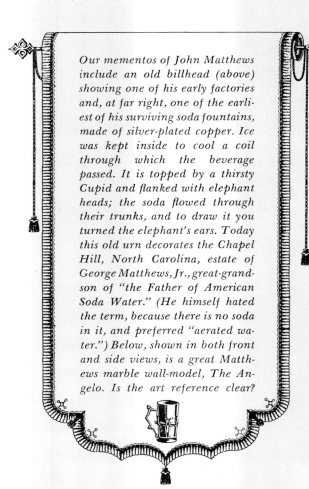

Our mementos of John Matthews include an old billhead (above) showing one of his early factories and, at far right, one of the earliest of his surviving soda fountains, made of silver-plated copper. Ice was kept inside to cool a coil through which the beverage passed. It is topped by a thirsty Cupid and flanked with elephant heads; the soda flowed through their trunks, and to draw it you turned the elephant's ears. Today this old urn decorates the Chapel Hill, North Carolina, estate of George Matthews, Jr., great-grandson of "the Father of American Soda Water." (He himself hated the term, because there is no soda in it, and preferred "aerated water.") Below, shown in both front and side views, is a great Matthews marble wall-model, The Angelo. Is the art reference clear?

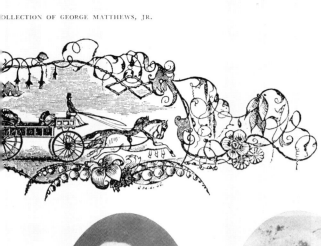

JOHN MATTHEWS:
He started it

BEN AUSTEN:
Human pressure gauge

GOOD HEAVENS FRIEND HOW CAN YOU WEAR AN OVERCOAT AND LOOK SO COOL THIS WARM WEATHER?
I ALWAYS BRING MY OVERCOAT DOWN TOWN, AS I FIND AFTER DRINKING A GLASS OF "BLAKELY'S BLIZZARD SODA," DRAWN FROM HIS "ARCTIC FOUNTAIN," THAT I AM COLD THE BALANCE OF THE DAY.

Byron loved soda water and so, it appears did Disraeli, for 4,000 empty bottles were found in his house when he died. There were all-male soda hangouts, as the extravagant 1890 advertisement at left indicates, but the better places strove to entice the ladies. The one at the right shows that as early as 1905, the Coca-Cola people were pushing their product hard. Invented by an Atlanta druggist in 1886, it became the greatest carbonated success of all time, and its claims, shown in the circle, were never modest.

In its heyday, an ornate art form grew up to supply the spreading soda fountain trade with dozens of new devices, from a two-dollar cup holder to the $500 decorative "cottage" fountain, below, patented in 1871, and always ready with ten delicious flavors.

In fact, hot water

Matthews' Change Holder

The Monitor, by the Tufts Company

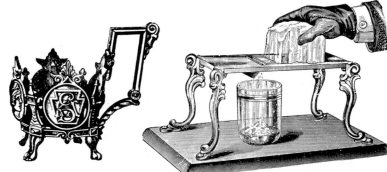

Spoon Holder

Tumbler Washer

Tumbler Holder

Ice Plane and Mitten

When it came to colored lithographs, it was hard to beat
A. D. Puffer & Sons, of Boston; this flight of fancy clearly
links the product to all that arctic ice, to a good many
races, to those happy monkeys, and even to the wise
old owl. Could that be the young John Glenn
beside him? The date: approximately 1875.

SODA

PUFFER'S
MAGIC FOUNTAIN

AMERICAN HERITAGE *is grateful to George Matthews, Jr., and John Poulos, making their collections of old catalogues and pictures available; and Miss Janice Devine and Leslie Dorsey for picture and caption research.*

As the nineteenth century wore on, all ages and classes seemed to have taken up ice cream and soda water. Witness these contrasting wood cuts, nabobs at the right, gamins to the left. In Once Upon a City, Grace Mayer quotes a 1901 newspaper on the phenomenon of the poor child with pocket money always ready for a soda. "Thriftless, but affectionate, is the lower class parent. Shoes the child must do without . . . But here is five cents to buy hokey-pokey. That much he can afford."

John Matthews, who started it all, believed in catching soda-water drinkers early, made a street dispensing cart, and waxed lyrical about his product: "Youth, as it sips its first glass, experiences sensations which, like the first sensations of love, cannot be forgotten but are cherished to the last." Who will argue with the old gentleman?

Finis

More than any other Civil War
general, says a distinguished
British critic, he grasped the
possibilities and requirements
of warfare in the modern age

Sherman—Modern Warrior

By CAPTAIN B. H. LIDDELL HART

The American Civil War produced nobody quite like William Tecumseh Sherman, the world's first modern "man of war." Not only was he a great commander; he also evolved fresh strategic techniques, and concepts developed from study of his operations had a far-reaching influence in the Second World War.

Sherman showed both the qualities and characteristics of genius. He was tall, lean, angular, loose-jointed, careless and unkempt in dress, with a restlessness of manner emphasized by his endless chain-smoking of cigars, and an insatiable curiosity, a raciness of language, and a fondness for picturesque phrases. But he was a blend of contrasting qualities. His dynamic energy went along with philosophical reflectiveness. He had faith in his own vision but a doubt of his own abilities that could only be dispelled gradually by actual achievement. He combined democratic tastes and manners with a deep and sardonic distrust of democracy. His rebelliousness was accompanied by a profound respect for law and order. His logical ruthlessness was coupled with compassion.

In generalship, he was brilliant, yet what made him outstanding was the way he came to see and exploit the changing conditions of warfare produced by mechanical and scientific developments.

The Civil War started with old-fashioned military concepts and weapons, but also with some very new instruments whose influence had not yet been realized.

Grim, unrelenting, and typically careless in his dress, William Tecumseh Sherman is shown here in a picture made at the close of the war. On his left sleeve is a band of crepe which he wore in mourning for the death of President Lincoln.

Until the middle of the nineteenth century, the means of movement had been unchanged throughout the ages. Armies marched on foot or horseback, and their supplies were carried in vehicles drawn by horses or oxen. At sea, they moved on sailing ships dependent on the wind. Even in the Napoleonic era the smoothbore musket and cannon were little more effective than the medieval bow and the ancient catapult. Means of communication were limited to messengers on horseback.

But by the time of the Civil War, new *mechanical* means of movement and communication had become available. This was the first war in which the railroad, the steamship, and the electric telegraph played an important part. Weapons had not changed so much, but the war speeded their development. The muzzle-loaded smoothbore musket was gradually replaced by a muzzle-loaded rifle, which was much more accurate. Breech-loading rifles came into use before the end of the war, and the increasing range and effect of fire made attack more difficult and costly. Troops were forced to take shelter in trenches or behind breastworks. *Tactical* movement, on the battlefield, easily became stagnant.

Meanwhile the large-scale transportation facilities offered by the railroads led commanders and governments to mass at the railheads larger forces than could be fed if the enemy cut the lines. These forces tended to become too massive to be maneuverable. Thus *strategic* movement was also inclined to become stagnant.

The combination produced a state of deadlock—even in the West, where space was wide and appeared to offer ample scope for maneuver. In 1862 and again in 1863, successive efforts by the Union forces to push southward were blocked or paralyzed by Confederate cavalry raids on the rail lines of supply.

A better way of tackling the problem was initiated by Grant's indirect approach to Vicksburg in the spring of 1863. Grant cut off this key point on the Mississippi by a wide circuit eastward and then northward, during which he momentarily cut loose from his line of supply. Sherman, then his principal executive, learned most from the bold experiment, becoming the first commander to show a clear grasp of the new conditions of warfare. At the start of the war he was still conventional in military outlook, but his civilian experience during the immediate prewar years, his unconventional character, and the experience of this Vicksburg campaign helped him to shake off the shackles of orthodoxy.

He could also see the significance of another important change—the growth of population and industrialization. This brought increased dependence on supplies, on manufactured weapons, and on means of communication—among which were newspapers, as well as transport and telegraph. This increased both the economic target and the moral target, and made both more vulnerable. This in turn increased the incentive to strike at the sources of the opponent's armed power instead of striking at its shield—the armed forces.

Sherman's grasp of this is very clearly shown in his letters and in his plans. Viewed in retrospect, it is evident that he was startlingly ahead of his time. Nearly half a century before the development of aircraft, his operations in the last year of the Civil War foreshadowed the aim and course pursued by the bomber offensive of World War II.

The dual influences of heredity and environment can be clearly traced in the molding of Sherman's character and outlook. He came from a Puritan family which had left England about 1634 to seek freedom of conscience and wider opportunity in the New World. The family moved first to Connecticut, and then to Ohio, where Charles Robert Sherman became a judge. Developing a deep admiration for the Indian chief Tecumseh, he had his third son, born on February 8, 1820, christened William Tecumseh Sherman.

The boy was left fatherless at the age of nine, but he was taken into the home of a friend, Senator Thomas Ewing, who helped him get an appointment to West Point when Sherman became sixteen. The four years there were purgatory, and it is evident that Sherman shared the feelings of Ulysses Grant, who wrote that the years "seemed about five times as long as Ohio years." Looking back, Sherman caustically remarked: "At the Academy I was not considered a good soldier, for at no time was I selected for any office. . . . Then, as now, neatness in dress and form, with a strict conformity, were the qualifications for office. . ." In studies Sherman ranked among the best, but he got so many demerits for nonconformity that he was in sixth place in the final class list.

Upon graduation, Sherman became an officer in the 3rd Artillery, in Florida, and he soon saw active service against the Seminole Indians. His letters to Ellen Ewing, the childhood playmate whom he subsequently married, show how much he enjoyed the excitement of the chase, but they also reveal his underlying sympathy with the chased, as well as his love of reading and of painting, his gift for writing, and his insatiable thirst for knowledge. They must sometimes have wearied a young girl thirsting for a more sentimental kind of communication.

Sherman missed the main action of the Mexican War, to his keen disappointment, through a posting to California, which he felt was a military backwater. But this widened his experience and eventually led to his being asked to return there, in 1853, as a working partner in a San Francisco banking house. He had married Ellen Ewing, and he was anxious to improve his family's prospects, so he quitted the Army at the age of thirty-three.

The boom was already subsiding, however, and many banks soon collapsed. In 1857 the parent bank in St. Louis was driven to suspend payment. That ended Sherman's banking career. He then joined a law firm at Leavenworth, Kansas, where his flair for topography made him valuable in surveying new areas and roads. But legal disputes were not to his taste, and in 1859 he jumped at a chance to become head of a new "Seminary and Military Academy" in Louisiana.

The new post provided ample scope for his energy and organizing power. He gained an impressive ascendancy over the hot-blooded southern cadets and also over the diverse elements among the board of supervisors. His personal popularity was the more remarkable because his brother John, who had been elected to Congress some years before, was regarded throughout the South as a "black Republican" and "awful abolitionist." Among his most staunch supporters were two of his future opponents on the battlefield, Braxton Bragg and P. G. T. Beauregard, who—by an irony of history—helped to dissuade him from accepting a tempting offer to go to England to represent a Cincinnati banking house in London, which would have removed the prospect of his playing a decisive part in the Civil War.

Sherman's letters in the summer of 1860 forecast that however "reasonable and moderate" Abraham Lincoln might be, in the South his name was like a red rag to

To Sherman, railroads were essential military objectives. This print shows his men at work during the march to the sea.

a bull, so that his election to the Presidency would make civil war likely—"reason has very little influence in this world; prejudice governs." As Sherman saw it, the basic objection to secession was the danger to the economy of the North that would arise from southern free trade and hostile control of the Mississippi.

On January 10, 1861, the United States Arsenal at Baton Rouge was surrounded—and surrendered—although Louisiana had not yet seceded. Sherman promptly resigned his office, but on returning to the North he was shocked by the complacency that prevailed. Disgusted with the politicians on both sides, Sherman felt inclined to stand aside and leave them to get out of the mess they had produced. He turned down an offer to make him Assistant Secretary of War, and when Lincoln called for 75,000 volunteers to serve for three months, Sherman's comment was: "You might as well attempt to put out the flames of a burning house with a squirt-gun." He wrote: "I think it is to be a long war—very long—much longer than any politician thinks." At the same time, he urged to his brother that "the questions of the national integrity and slavery should be kept distinct, for otherwise it will gradually become a war of extermination—a war without end."

It was only when Lincoln decided to increase the Regular Army and called on men to volunteer for three years of duty that Sherman offered his services. He was given command of a brigade in the hastily improvised force of 30,000 men that marched out from Washington in July to tackle the Confederates at the First Bull Run. When this battle ended in a Union defeat, Sherman distinguished himself in covering the disorderly retreat and checking the pursuers. But as the retreat continued, even his regiments dissolved into the general stream of fugitives, and he bitterly reported that the whole army "has degenerated into an armed mob."

When the President drove round the camps, Sherman pointedly asked him to discourage all cheering, and told him that "what we needed were cool, thoughtful, hard-fighting soldiers—no more hurrahing, no more humbug." Lincoln took the rebuke in good part. When one of the officers complained that Sherman had threatened to shoot him for defiance of orders, Lincoln replied with a twinkle: "Well, if I were you and he threatened to shoot, I wouldn't trust him, for I believe he would do it."

As soon as it became clear that no immediate Confederate advance on Washington was likely, Sherman

CONTINUED ON PAGE 102

23

"My beloued and good Husband..."

Thus Margaret Winthrop to her spouse, the governor of the Bay Colony. Her letters—and John's in reply—reveal behind the cold Puritan exterior a warm and deeply touching relationship

By DARRETT B. RUTMAN

I have many resons to make me love thee whereof I will name two," Margaret Winthrop once wrote her husband. "First because thou lovest God, and secondly because that thou lovest me. If these two were wantinge all the rest would be eclipsed."

The year was 1627, nine years after the marriage of John and Margaret Winthrop, three years before John was to lead the first major wave of Puritan migration to Massachusetts Bay in the New World, and more than four years before Margaret was to leave the comforts and relative riches of an English manor house to follow her husband to the wilds of America. In England in that year of 1627, King Charles I was fighting Parliament tooth and nail, levying a "forced loan" to circumvent Parliament's self-asserted right to the exclusive establishment of taxes and imprisoning landholders who refused to "lend" the monarch what he wanted. The Puritan revolt—half religious, half parliamentary—which would end in regicide and Oliver Cromwell, was in the making. Puritan men were being branded as "illiterate, morose, melancholy, discontented, crazed"; the Puritan woman was being lampooned in a popular book of the day as "a she-precise hypocrite" who "overflows so with the Bible that she spills it upon every occasion, and will not cudgel her maids without Scripture." John Winthrop, on business in London, surrounded by heated partisanship, could find relief in the quiet words of home and love: "But I must leave this discourse and go about my household affayres. I am a bad huswife to be so longe from them; but I must needs borowe a little time to talke with thee my sweet harte."

Except that she was John Winthrop's wife, history knows little of Margaret. Before their marriage, John was a dour, morbid, introspective, and hyperintense Puritan, converted to his ways by his first wife, made desolate by the death of his second after only a year of marriage. Afterward, in England and as governor of Puritan Massachusetts, he was gentle, considerate, kind, and even liberal in his dealings with the non-Puritan world. Margaret has been given credit for the transformation. But no portrait of her exists, no description other than John's sometime comments on her

Opposite: Margaret Winthrop's writing table might have looked much like this, with a family Bible open before her, a Van Dyck miniature of her beloved husband nearby, a quill and inkstand ready at hand. The letter is an actual one written in the early summer of 1628, when John was in London attending to his legal practice and she was at Groton caring for their growing family. All the objects here are Winthrop heirlooms in the collection of the Massachusetts Historical Society in Boston, where—with the Society's cooperation—Geoffrey Clements recently photographed them.

as "a very gracious woman" of "sweet face" and "lovely countenance" surrounded by "sweet and smiling" children.

We do know that she was born in 1591 at Chelmshey House, Great Maplestead, not far from the Winthrop family home, Groton, in Suffolk. Her father was Sir John Tyndal, knight and judge of chancery court. There, in a farm-and-gentry environment much like that in which John was raised, Margaret learned her letters, undoubtedly from her mother, Anne, who introduced her to the complexities of running a seventeenth-century household, perhaps even reading to her the poetic proscriptions of neighbor Thomas Tusser's *Booke of Huswiferie:*

> *Though cat (a good mouser) doth dwell in the house*
> *yet ever in dairy have trap for a mouse.*
> *Take heed how thou layest the bane for the rats*
> *for poisoning of servant, thyself and thy brats.*
> *Though scouring be needful, yet scouring too much*
> *is pride without profit and robbeth thine hutch.*
> *The woman the name of a huswife doth win,*
> *by keeping her house, and of doings therein;*
> *And she that with husband will quietly dwell*
> *must think in this lesson, and follow it well.*

From child, to girl, to woman. At twenty-six, tragedy struck Margaret when her father was murdered by a disappointed litigant. But on May 17, 1617, John Winthrop, tall and bearded, with piercing eyes and a wistful expression, looking younger than his twenty-nine years, came calling for the first time, riding down from Groton to pay his respects and charm the daughter of the house. Where the two had met, or if they had met at all before this visit, is unknown. What is certain is that John began courting her a bare five months after the death of his second wife. On April 24, 1618, after Margaret had overcome the scruples of her family, who thought him not well enough off to support her, John took her home to Groton as his wife.

A bride at twenty-seven—old for an east-country girl to be just married—Margaret was bright and sparkling, vivacious; willful, but retiring too, as befitted a country daughter and wife of that time; apparently Puritan but not nearly as religious-minded as her husband. An overfondness for clothes, for doodads and spangles, had brought a sharp warning from John in one of two letters surviving from the courtship. Putting the blame not on her but on relatives "savouring too much of the flesh," John had taken pains to point out that "ornaments which for virgins and knights' daughters, *et cetera* may be comely" hardly suited a Puritan wife. Pert Margaret complied and dressed from then on in blacks and grays and olive greens. But as a husband, John found himself buying an inordinate number of dresses, gowns, petticoats, and velvet capes.

Only in the matter of dress does there seem to have been difficulty in Margaret's change to Groton, the house that John's grandfather had bought and which she now called home. Set on a rise overlooking the five hundred acres of the estate and, in the distance, the River Box and the neighboring village of Boxford, Groton Manor was not opulent. But its hall and great parlor, its many chambers, its pantry, buttery, bakehouse, and brewing house were ample. So too were the produce of the garden that fed the family, and the income of the dependent farms, part from crops and part from the rent of tenants, which when combined with John's income as a lawyer gave them some eighty pounds a year. Within a few years, as John advanced in his profession and inherited the remainder of his father's estate, his income was to climb to seven hundred pounds.

At Chelmshey, children and guests had filled the house, their care and comfort being the province of Margaret and her mother. Now there was the same flurry at Groton, where Margaret found herself the mother of four children by John's first wife: John, Jr., Henry, Forth, and Mary. She herself was to bear John eight of her own: Stephen within a year, Adam, Deane, and Samuel; four others died in infancy. Nine servants or more; her mother-in-law, Anne; and John's unmarried sister, Lucy, lived in the house, too. And there was John's father, Adam, he who welcomed her to the family as "gentle mistress Margaret" and who wrote gay doggerel to her:

> The sweetness of your love
> Which I did lately taste,
> Doth make me to affect the same,
> Even with a mind most chaste
>
> For though my youth be past
> And head is clad with gray,
> Yet in your love I do rejoice
> As do the birds in May.

But if the house was crowded with relatives and visitors—the Winthrop clan was large, and Puritan "brothers" and "sisters" were always welcome—it was all too often empty for the bride. As a lawyer, John's work took him regularly to London, leaving Margaret busy but lonely at Groton. Letters passing between the two give a portrait that belies the coldness usually attributed to the Puritans.

Mundane matters take up much of these letters. There are the errands that John must do for her in London, clothes he must buy, tobacco that his mother wants him to bring back for her. There is the "turkey and two capons and a cheese" that Margaret is always sending to him, the family greetings that must be passed on, the pipe that John is giving up, the caution against "taking cold." There are sick servants and sick children to report. There is coy confession, a trip Margaret takes without John's knowledge or permission: "Thou seest how bold I am to take leave to go abroad in thy absence, but I presume upon thy love and consent, or else I would not do it." * There is talk of the wayward son, Henry. There are religious exhortations from John, too, and once Margaret responds: "Those serious thoughts of your own which you sent me did make a very good supply instead of a sermon." But above all, these are love letters:

My good husband, your love to me doth daily give me cause of comfort, and doth much increase my love to you, for love liveth by love. I were worse than a brute beast if I should not love and be faithful to thee who hath deserved so well at my hands. I am ashamed and grieved with myself that I have nothing within or without worthy of thee, and yet it pleaseth thee to except of both and to rest contented. . . .

I am much indebted to you for your loving and long letters that I must needs write a word or two to show my thankfulness and kind acceptance of them, although I can do nothing to equal them or to requite your love; and so I think I had better do a little than not at all, that I may show my willingness to do it though I am ashamed I can do no better. . . .

What can be more pleasing to a wife, than to hear of the welfare of her best beloved, and how he is pleased with her poor endeavors. I blush to hear myself commended, knowing my own wants; but it is your love that conceives the best and makes all things seem better than they are. I wish that I may be always pleasing to thee, and that those comforts we have in each other may be daily increased as far as they be pleasing to God. I will use that speech to thee that Abigail did to David: I will be a servant to wash the feet of my Lord; I will do any service wherein I may please my good husband. I confess I cannot do enough for thee, but thou art pleased to accept the will for the deed and rest contented.

Your loving and obedient wife

In London, or on occasional trips elsewhere, John read her letters, and, as he had done in the days of their courtship when he wrote "to my best beloved, Mistress Margaret Tyndal," he answered in kind:

And now, my sweet love, let me a while solace myself in the remembrance of our love, of which this springtime of our acquaintance can put forth as yet no more but the leaves and blossoms whilst the fruit lies wrapped up in the tender bud of hope. . . . Let it be our care and labor to preserve these hopeful buds from the beasts of the field, and from frosts and other injuries of the air, lest our fruit fall off ere it be ripe, or lose aught in the beauty and pleasantness of it. . . .

I must intreat thy gentle patience until this business be

* The previous quotations from Margaret Winthrop's letters to her husband in London have been reproduced with the original spellings and punctuation unchanged. In this one and those following, they have been modernized: the vagaries of seventeenth-century orthography often obscure the meaning.—*Editor*

dispatched, which I hope will be betimes the next week. In the meantime, thou art well persuaded that my heart is with thee, as (I know) thine is with him to whom thou has given thyself, a faithful and loving yokel. . . .

I thank thee for thy kind letters, but I know not what to say for myself. I should mend and grow a better husband, having the help and example of so good a wife, but I grow still worse. . . .

Thou mayest marvel that thou had no letter from me . . . but I know thou wilt not impute it to any decay of love or neglect of thee, who art more precious to me than any other thing in this world.

                    Thy frail yet faithful husband.

During the dozen years the couple lived in England there was no diminishment. Taking a moment here and there—she from her housework, he usually late at night—the two wrote often and ardently. When John fell ill in London and told Margaret to stay at Groton, she disregarded his words about the difficulty of winter travel and went to him. John hurt his hand, and Margaret wrote in sympathy: "I will not look for any long letters this term because I pity your poor hand. If I had it here I would make more of it than ever I did, and bind it up very softly for fear of hurting it." Writing on a fourteenth of February, John scrawled a postscript: "Thou must be my valentine, for none hath challenged me."

Only occasionally did John mention contemporary happenings in his letters, and then in bare, stark terms: "Two or three Londoners committed about the loan"; "News from Bohemia is very bad"; "The gentlemen who were in prison are like to be delivered." But behind these few comments is the history of a decade of turbulence both in England and on the Continent. In Europe, ablaze with the Thirty Years' War, Protestantism seemed to be crumbling before the Catholic Counter Reformation. Cardinal Richelieu, in France, had besieged and conquered the Huguenot stronghold at La Rochelle; in Protestant Germany, Wallenstein was cutting his bloody swath in the name of Catholicism. And in England there was growing tenseness between Puritans and emerging Anglicanism, between Parliament and King. Religion and politics had become hopelessly intertwined as Charles I insisted on religious conformity and parliamentary subservience, while Puritans sought a strong Parliament as protection for their religious views. In March of 1629 a crisis was reached when Parliament decreed that supporters of the royal prerogative and the High Church were enemies of the realm. Charles retaliated in a climactic and violent scene, closing Parliament and trundling its Puritan leaders off to the Tower of London.

To John Winthrop—made vaguely discontented throughout the preceding decade by what he consid-ered a religiously "desolate" country, by a Catholic queen, by the genuflection and high altar of the Anglican Church, by the corruption and immorality of the Stuart kings—the closing of Parliament seemed disastrous. Combined with the rise to power of Bishop William Laud, archexponent of the High Church, and a wave of anti-Puritan persecution, it portended the subjugation of Puritanism in England, perhaps even England's return to Catholicism and a repetition of the bloodletting of La Rochelle and Germany.

From London during the feverish days that followed the closing of Parliament, John unburdened himself to Margaret. We can almost hear his panic when, in May, 1629, he wrote to her condemning his own past complacency and passiveness in "these so evil and declining times" and expressing dread for the future. The Protestant churches of Europe had been "smitten," he wrote; the Lord had

made them to drink of the bitter cup of tribulation, even unto death; we saw this, and humbled not ourselves to turn from our evil ways, but hath provoked Him more than all the nations around us.
Therefore He is turning the cup toward us also, and because we are the last, our portion must be to drink the very dregs which remain.
My dear wife, I am verily persuaded God will bring some heavy affliction upon this land, and that speedily.

His composure had slipped for a moment but had not been lost. In the same letter John could assure Margaret that in the catastrophe which seemed so imminent, "He will provide a shelter and a hiding place for us and ours, as a Zoar for Lott." And when, during the surge of Puritan persecution, John lost his position with the Court of Wards and Liveries which had taken him so often to London, he could offer her consolation in the fact that, as he wrote, "I shall not wrong thee so much with my absence as I have done."

Whatever joy Margaret had in this promise was doomed to quick disappointment, however, for the loss of his position freed John for the project of planting a Puritan refuge—the "hiding place" he had written of earlier—in the New World. Not only would this entail a separation of more than a year, but eventually Margaret would have to give up Groton and sail overseas herself. John seems to have asked her if she would do this, and though the reply is missing, she undoubtedly answered in biblical terms: "Whither thou goest, I will go." "My comfort," he wrote her, "is that thou art willing to be my companion in what place or condition soever, in weal or woe." John sent her pamphlets and letters describing New England, which she read and "rejoiced" in. She had no misgivings about the project, she told him, but in his letters John seemed

CONTINUED ON PAGE 94

LITH & PRINTED IN TINTS BY SARONY & MAJOR, NEW YORK.

CHANG AND ENG, THE WORLD RENOWNED SIAMESE TWI

*A florid mid-nineteenth-century poster depicted the twins,
their wives, and some of their progeny. Surrounding vi-
gnettes presented a fanciful tableau of their daily lives.*

World-famous as medical curiosities, the original Siamese twins married,

brought up families, and, as American citizens,

became prosperous planters in the Old South

Never Alone at Last

By JONATHAN DANIELS

WIVES AND CHILDREN,

The strangest romance in the annals of the Old South culminated in North Carolina, not many miles west of modern Winston-Salem, in 1843, when Chang and Eng Bunker, slaveholders and adoptive southerners, married Sarah Ann and Adelaide Yeats, daughters of a Virginia clergyman. It was by necessity a double ceremony.

Today the memory of the bridegrooms is celebrated by a double headstone over their single grave in the cemetery of the Baptist church of White Plains, North Carolina. From great quarries nearby, granite has gone to mark many other graves and to build such monuments as the Wright Memorial at Kitty Hawk and the Arlington Memorial Bridge across the Potomac. But Chang and Eng's real monument is not of the familiar Carolina granite, though it may one day prove as enduring. It is the term "Siamese twins."

Doctors still deal with cases of twins whose bodies are joined together—described rather roughly in the dictionary as a "double monster." Newspapers and medical journals in recent years have reported successful and unsuccessful efforts to separate such twins, some of whom have qualified for the cruel epithet "monster." Certainly, however, a century and a half after the birth of the original Siamese twins, it still seems strange to apply the word to that gay, shrewd, acquisitive, lively, and fertile pair who made their way before an astonished world from Siam to plantations in Surry County, North Carolina. Their lives were almost as dramatic as their deaths.

Chang and Eng were born near Bangkok, the capital of Siam, on the river Me Nam, in May, 1811. Bangkok then was a city built largely on floating pontoons or on piles; in the stagnant, dry season the death rate was high, especially among children, but Chang and Eng thrived. They seemed not at all disturbed by the stout attachment of cartilage and ligaments that joined them together at the breastbone. At first this fleshy tie was short and rigid, but as they grew, the ligament stretched so that they could stand side by side and even back to back.

They also ran, jumped, and swam with ease and astounding co-ordination. Indeed, their activities in the water drew them to the attention of Robert Hunter, a British merchant in Siam. At first he thought he had encountered some strange amphibious animal. Soon, however, he realized that here was a human wonder that would appeal to the curiosity of the Western world and might put more money in his pocket than he was making in Asian trade.

In April, 1829, the twins, accompanied by Hunter, sailed from Siam on an American ship, the *Sachem*. They arrived in Boston on August 16 "in excellent health." The United States was then already a land of people eager to confront wonders and sometimes to be fooled. When the eighteen-year-old twins reached America, Phineas T. Barnum, "the greatest American showman," who was to present them later along with other freaks, real and false, was himself only nineteen. However, Chang and Eng, the first genuine xiphopagic twins (as doctors called them) ever seen here, required no genius as showmen to attract great popular and medical interest.

They were already accustomed to the latter. Back in Siam some native doctors had proposed plans for separating the boys. One suggested "hanging them across a fine cat-gut cord, like a pair of saddle-bags, estimating that this would, in time, work its way entirely through the connecting ligature, by degrees, allowing the several parts to heal as it progressed." Another advised cutting them apart with a red-hot wire. But in the United States, eminent doctors were less inclined to advise such measures.

John Collins Warren, then professor of anatomy and surgery in the Harvard Medical School, made careful studies of the twins. He concluded that the band between them was largely cartilage with an insignificant number of connecting blood vessels, lymphatics, and small nerves. He felt, however, that there was probably a continuous peritoneal cavity within the band which would make attempts at surgical separation hazardous and unwarranted. Other leading American physicians concurred. For Chang and Eng it was probably just as well; if they had been separated, they would have gained comfort and independence, but they would have been reduced to two lonely and insignificant Siamese boys, stranded far from home.

So, still joined, they sailed from the United States to England, where they were enthusiastically welcomed in October of 1829. Crowds poured out to see them, and once again the doctors examined them. Sir Astley Paston Cooper, president of the Royal College of Surgeons, also held back from the suggestion that the twins be separated.

Other medical reports were made. Sir James Y. Simpson, then only beginning his great career as a Scottish physician, found that when potassium iodide was given to one twin no iodide reaction was found in the urine of his partner. In a study more comprehensible to the layman, Professor G. B. Bolton fed asparagus to Chang and found its characteristic odor in his urine, but none in Eng's. The doctors considered it significant that though Chang began to drink heavily as time went on, Eng was never affected even when his brother was drunk.

If the pushing, shoving, and curious stares of the crowds and the thumping and probing of the doctors disturbed the brothers, they certainly were not displeased by the money which poured in. All of it belonged to them once they had reached the age of twenty-one and had dispensed with the services of their "owner," Hunter. By 1833, they had amassed a fortune of some $60,000, and they decided to retire. After a little more than four years as famous freaks, they were world-renowned. They had not only advertised Siam, but they also constituted about all the civilized world knew of their homeland.

They returned to the United States, cut off the queues they had earlier worn, and became both naturalized American citizens and Baptists. They assumed the surname of Bunker. According to one story, they took it from a bystander at the immigration office when they were told they must have a family name. Another version is that they adopted the name Bunker (North Carolina corruption of Bon Coeur) from a friend in that state. At any event, when they settled there, the legislature allowed them to take the name.

They made their home near the town of Mt. Airy in Surry County, in the northwestern part of the state, and soon established themselves as prosperous and competent farmers. They were welcomed there. Tired of travel, they found the forested hill country appealing. It was no tidewater area of settled gentility but more like the frontier, a place in which men noted that with their four arms the twins made "excellent hands to carry up the corner of a loghouse" (as their authorized literary promoter put it). Each of them could use an axe at the same time without interfering with the other. Sometimes they swung one axe with all arms. With two axes they could cut from the opposite sides of a tree, bringing it down in short order.

Because they were "sensitive" men "disposed to

Late in life, Eng (left) and Chang (right) sat with their wives and two sons for the photographer Mathew Brady. Here the connecting band of flesh and cartilage can be plainly seen.

shun observation," they "selected so retired a portion of the country for their residence." But they were hardly recluses. They had learned to speak English well by the time they arrived in North Carolina—perhaps from answering the questions of the curious who examined them. They had also learned the value of the dollar. With their savings they acquired a plantation with slaves and livestock. Later, after their marriages, they built a house in Mt. Airy itself so that their children might be near a school. Their back-country neighbors regarded them as "remarkable for their energy and industry" and their frugal manner of living. Those neighbors learned, too, that "in point of shrewdness in a trade" the twins were a match for anyone. In business deals, they were always partners and "in signing papers, one always signed for both."

Though retired, the twins did not relish a life of inactivity. Excellent judges of horseflesh, they could tame the wildest colts. They could do more actual labor than any four slaves. Still, despite their disposition to shun the vulgar curiosity of crowds, both Chang and Eng were friendly, even gregarious, neighbors in the back country. Familiarity made them seem less freakish there. Respect for them grew after they killed a marauding wolf, known far and wide as "Bobtail," which had terrorized the region by carrying off not only sheep, calves, and swine but, it was said, Negro babies as well.

The brothers became, like their neighbors, inveterate smokers and chewers of tobacco. They were regular attendants at church and other religious meetings. They joined their neighbors in fishing, hunting, and games—and while they played chess and draughts "tolerably well," they got no enjoyment from playing each other. They joined in the lively interest of Carolinians in politics and took part in all elections in their district; it is not in the record as to whether they agreed or disagreed on political matters. Yet the Siamese strangers in Carolina sometimes quarreled with each other so violently that once they begged their family physician, Dr. Joseph Hollingsworth, to cut them apart, even if it killed them. As time went on, Chang grew more irritable and more attached to the bottle.

In 1853, after nearly twenty years of busy retirement, the twins took to the road again, announcing "their intention of exhibiting themselves once more, during a very brief period, after which it is their firm determination to take their final retirement from public life." Possibly a little traveling circus which passed by their property—the sight of an elephant trudging through back-country Carolina set all the dogs howling—made them long for the excitements of the tent and the museum.

More probably marriage and growing families made it necessary. Ultimately Chang had ten children by

CONTINUED ON PAGE 106

*Charles Willson Peale painted this portrait of Benjamin Henry Latrobe
about the time of the architect's marriage, in Philadelphia, in 1800.
It may have been a wedding portrait; in any case it shows him at the
height of his early success in America—the much-admired designer of
the Bank of Pennsylvania and engineer of the Philadelphia waterworks.*

32

The great public buildings of a restless genius
helped shape the face of his adopted country,
and his journals, letters, and sketches bril-
liantly caught the spirit of the young nation

Latrobe's America

By PAUL F. NORTON and E. M. HALLIDAY

Thomas Jefferson was impatient. Work on the United States Capitol had been progressing only fitfully since George Washington had approved the architectural plans in 1793; and now, in the fall of 1803, things seemed to be moving at a glacial pace. The north wing, to be sure, had been finished for several years and was in use by the Senate—in fact, the floor beams were already beginning to rot and the roof leaked badly. Meanwhile the south wing, intended for the House of Representatives, existed only as a crude temporary structure built on a more or less permanent base; and the middle section was just a confused network of uncompleted foundations. In March, 1803, President Jefferson had appointed a new architect to push the work along; yet here it was November and nothing palpable had been accomplished.

In this irritating situation, and with Congress grumbling bitterly about the delays, Jefferson—himself an amateur architect—made what he thought was a constructive suggestion. Why not, he said, build the great columns for the House of Representatives out of wood? It would be cheaper, and above all it would be quicker than waiting for the stonecutters to hew the massive stone segments which the architect had called for.

But Jefferson had figured without fully knowing the temper of the man he had recently employed.

The Maryland Historical Society has recently acquired an extraordinary historical treasure: 8,800 letters, 325 paintings and drawings, and 14 diaries, all from the hand of Benjamin Henry Latrobe. James W. Foster, director of the Society from 1942 until his unexpected death last spring, devoted much time to securing the collection, which he described as "without parallel in this country." This article is based in part on a study of the Maryland Latrobe collection; and most of the color portfolio beginning on page 41 is drawn from it by special arrangement with the Society.

"The wooden column idea," the architect declared in a hasty message to his chief assistant, "is one with which I never will have anything to do. On that you may rely. I will give up my office sooner than build a temple of disgrace to myself and Mr. Jefferson."

The man whose stubborn integrity envisioned a United States Capitol as enduring as the Constitution that it symbolized was Benjamin Henry Latrobe. An American only since 1796, when he had voyaged to Virginia from England, he had wholeheartedly adopted the new nation as his own, and was on the way to becoming the most influential architect and engineer of its adolescent years.

Yet Latrobe's contribution to United States culture did not end with the many structures, public and private, that he designed and built. A man of quick sensibility and intense curiosity, he has left us, besides, a uniquely evocative panorama of early America as he saw and recorded it in hundreds of sketches, water colors, letters, and painstakingly kept journals.

Adversity brought Benjamin Latrobe to America, as it brought thousands of others before and after. At twenty-eight he was one of London's most promising young architects, with a lovely wife and two children; the future looked good. At twenty-nine he was unemployed, a widower, and in political disfavor. Architectural commissions had dwindled disastrously with the outbreak of war between England and France in 1793, and Latrobe's French name and known approval of the French Revolution did not help matters. Then, in the fall of 1793, his young wife died in childbirth.

Latrobe tried for two years to recoup his fortune, but with little luck. Morose over the loss of his wife, he fell into gloomy ways which decreased the already scant demand for his skills. Finally he decided on a fresh start: he would try America. His mother was an American who had come from Pennsylvania to study in an English Moravian school and remained to marry a Moravian minister; her son Benjamin was born on May 1, 1764. She not only had taught him much about the colonies, but had left him some American real estate. With an excellent continental education and several years' professional experience behind him, Latrobe had every reason to expect that his architectural talents would be valuable in the new republic across the Atlantic. He left his infant children in the care of relatives and took passage near the close of 1795.

*L*anding in Norfolk in mid-March, 1796, Latrobe plunged into an effort to become acquainted with the country. It was an era when men of culture and intellect easily met others of their kind if they could surmount practical obstacles. By dint of cheerful travel, mostly on horseback over muddy roads, Latrobe met and conversed with scores of eminent Virginians before he had been in America six months. The Pennocks, the Skipwiths, the Blackburns, the Randolphs, the Bushrod Washingtons—all were his hosts, and all found him charming and extraordinarily gifted. He sketched and painted, he wrote poetry, he displayed his various musical and linguistic abilities; and he designed an elegant house—his first in America —for Captain Pennock, of Norfolk. At the same time he kept up his journal, filling it with penetrating observations on the look of the countryside, the character of the great houses (he found them shabby by European standards), and the demeanor of American women (he found them lovely and unaffected).

As always throughout his life, Latrobe's remarks in his journals and letters reveal a man whose human sympathy nicely balanced his almost scientific devotion to facts. Having declared that the mansions of Virginia were shabby, he observes: "It is a necessary consequence of the remoteness of the country. . . . An unlucky boy breaks two or three squares of glass. The glazier lives fifty miles off. An old newspaper supplies their place in the *mean time*. Before the *mean time* is over the family gets used to the newspapers & think no more of the glazier." And speaking (to an imaginary correspondent) of the Virginia ladies, he is moved to further social comment:

I prefer their manners without exception to those of the Women of any country I was ever in. Were I to chuse a Wife by manners I would chuse a Virginian, and yet let me tell you there are things done & seen in Virginia which would shock the delicacy of a bold Englishwoman . . . What think you of the known promiscuous intercourse of your servants, the perpetual pregnancies of your young servant girls, fully exhibited to your children . . .

Oh but who minds the blacks . . . You are right, Madam! Poor wretched Blacks! You are indeed degraded: not even considered as better for virtue, or worse for vice! Outcasts of the moral, as of the political world!

Progressively furnished with cordial letters of introduction, the young architect jogged the back roads from plantation to plantation, sometimes making visits of unusual interest for the annals of American history. He happened to arrive at Bizarre, the estate of Richard Randolph, during the final episode of the strange and violent *ménage à trois* which had developed between that gentleman, his wife, Judith, and her beautiful sister, Nancy (see Francis Biddle's "Scandal at Bizarre" in the August, 1961, AMERICAN HERITAGE). Latrobe found Richard Randolph acutely sick with what appeared to be an attack of indigestion— since diagnosed by many researchers as poisoning at the hands of the jealous Judith. The embarrassed guest stayed one night and left in the morning, thus missing Richard Randolph's death by a few hours.

It was shortly after this that he visited Mount Vernon. George Washington, less than a generation after his famous exploits as leader of the Revolution, had already attained an almost mythological stature among his countrymen, and of this Latrobe was well aware. He came prepared to exhibit the best deportment of an English gentleman, but to watch, listen, and make notes with the scrupulous attention of a star reporter. Bushrod Washington, the great man's nephew, had written a letter of introduction for him, and on July 17, 1796, he trotted his horse up the country road to Mount Vernon:

The house becomes visible between two groves of trees at about a mile's distance. . . . Everything . . . is extremely good & neat, but by no means above what would be expected in a plain English country gentleman's house of £500 or £600 a year. . . .

Having alighted at Mount Vernon, I sent in my letter of introduction, and walked into the portico next to the river. In about 10 minutes the President came to me. He was dressed in a plain blue coat, his hair dressed & powdered. There was a reserve but no hauteur in his manner.

An hour's conversation ensued in which the President made precise comments about high life at Bath (now Berkeley Springs, West Virginia), the various rivers of Virginia, the Dismal Swamp, and canal building.

Since Washington had at first remarked that he was in process of finishing some letters to go by the next mail, Latrobe now rose to leave; but evidently he had by this time charmed his host: "He desired me, in a manner very like Dr. Johnson's, to 'keep my chair,' and then continued to talk to me." They covered architectural projects in England, Latrobe's family connections in Pennsylvania, and coal mines. Latrobe mentioned the possibility of silver mining in Virginia. To this Washington replied that he "heartily wished for his country that it might contain *no mines but such as the plow could reach, excepting only coal and iron.*" Then he got up and left his guest, saying that they would meet again at dinner.

Accepting the implied invitation, Latrobe went out and prowled about the grounds, making sketches to serve as the basis for later water colors. When he went back to the house, he met Mrs. Washington and her granddaughter, both of whom he found attractive:

[Mrs. Washington] retains strong remains of considerable beauty, seems to enjoy very good health, & to have as good humor. She has no affectation of superiority in the slightest degree, but acts completely in the character of the mistress of the house of a respectable and opulent country gentleman. Her granddaughter, Miss Eleanor Custis (the only one of four who is unmarried) has more perfection of form, of expression, of color, of softness, and of firmness of mind than I have ever seen before, or conceived consistent with mortality. She is everything that the chisel of Phidias aimed at but could not reach . . .

They were soon joined by young George Washington Lafayette, son of the famous French general, who was staying with the Washingtons during his father's imprisonment in Austria. It was now midafternoon, and President Washington reappeared for dinner.

The meal itself Latrobe found rather stiff:

There was very little conversation. . . . A few jokes passed between the President and young Lafayette, whom he treats more as his child than as a guest. [Lafayette was seventeen at the time.] I felt a little embarrassed at the silent, reserved air that prevailed. As I drink no wine, and the President drank only three glasses, the party soon returned to the portico. . . . The President retired in about ¾ of an hour.

Again, not wishing to exhaust his welcome, Latrobe prepared to leave and had actually ordered his horse to the door when Washington came to him and asked whether he departed upon "any very pressing business." Latrobe said no, but that he did not wish to intrude upon the President's more important affairs.

"Sir," said Washington, "you see I take my own way. If you can be content to take yours at my house, I shall be glad to see you here longer."

So Latrobe stayed for the night. Coffee was served

Endowed with a vivid sense of history, Latrobe put it to good use at Mount Vernon by sketching whenever he got the chance. His candid profile of Washington (right) was "stolen" without the General's knowledge. The group on the veranda, below, includes the lovely Eleanor Custis (Martha Washington's granddaughter), a servant, Martha, and the young son of one of her husband's secretaries.

about six o'clock, and Washington then again engaged his guest in conversation on a wide scope of topics—most of them, however, of an agricultural color. There is just a suspicion that Latrobe was a little bored: "He gave me a very minute account of the Hessian fly and its progress from Long Island, where it first appeared, through New York, Rhode Island, Connecticut, Delaware, part of Pennsylvania, & Maryland. It has not yet appeared in Virginia, but is daily dreaded." The talk droned on while the summer darkness fell; and about 8 P.M., the ladies having already vanished, Washington surprised Latrobe by bidding him good-night and going off, evidently to bed. The young architect, who by this time would have been gratified at the sight of food, was left to be conducted by a servant to his chamber. On what can only be presumed to have been a rather hollow note, he inscribed in his journal: "There was no hint of supper."

Arising with the sun, possibly as a result of hunger, Latrobe went out and again walked the grounds of Mount Vernon. When he returned, "The President came to the company in the sitting room about ½ hour past seven, where all the latest newspapers were laid out. . . . Breakfast was served up in the usual Virginia style. Tea, coffee, and cold & broiled meat. It was very soon over, & for an hour afterwards, he stood upon the steps of the west door talking to the company who were collected around him. The subject was chiefly the establishment of the University at the Federal City [Washington, D.C.]."

The visit ended shortly after that. Latrobe noted later in his journal: "On the morning of my departure he treated me as if I had lived for years in his house, with ease and attention, but . . . I thought there was a slight air of moroseness about him, as if something had vexed him."

Acquaintance with some of the leading figures of the day brought Latrobe professional work as well as numerous social engagements. Settling in Richmond, he was soon enormously busy—designing homes, attending parties, painting the water colors of which he was so fond, courting young ladies with impromptu poetry, even writing a comedy for a popular actress of the day who had caught his fancy. (He reports that he wrote the play in twenty-six hours—and it survived not much longer than that, for the theatre burned down after one performance—"a judgment on the house for the prostitution committed on the stage," according to an unfriendly critic.)

This early period of Latrobe's Americanization also saw the first of his public works in this country. It was a prison—not a likely project, one might think, for his benevolent temperament; but in fact the Richmond penitentiary showed in its design many features which were humane innovations in accord with the new views of crime and punishment advanced by Thomas Jefferson. Latrobe won the commission by competition, and his design was duly carried out, but he had trouble collecting his fee—an ominous foreshadowing of business frustrations which would plague him until his death.

A visit to Philadelphia in the spring of 1798 convinced Latrobe that this, the exciting and wealthy capital of the young country, was the best place for his activities. Dining one evening with the president

of the Bank of Pennsylvania, he quickly sketched a plan for a new bank building which was so impressive that, a few months later, Latrobe was asked to come and work out a full design. By Christmas of 1798 he was happily settled as a Philadelphia resident, and hard at work.

Never a man to do just one thing at a time, Latrobe no sooner got started on the plans for the Bank of Pennsylvania than he dove into the middle of a controversy about Philadelphia's water supply. The growing city still depended on shallow wells, and these were so contaminated by sewage that a drink of clean, good-tasting water was scarcely to be had anywhere in the central part of town. The obvious source of good water was the Schuylkill, but getting it out of the river was a problem. A group of Philadelphians had formed a company to bring it into the city by gravity, through a four-mile aqueduct leading from the falls north of the city. Upon this plan Latrobe cast the skeptical eye of a man well-trained in engineering as well as architecture. He found it full of technical faults, and he countered with a radical proposal: take the water from the Schuylkill just outside Philadelphia, and achieve the necessary pressure with steam pumps. Rapidly he drew up a detailed outline of his scheme and presented it to the city council.

Despite violent verbal assaults from the aqueduct company—accusing Latrobe of greed, incompetence, alcoholism, and a highly suspicious foreign background—the city fathers saw the functional beauty of his plan, and he was appointed city engineer to carry it out. Months of difficulty followed, yet by January, 1801, the system was ready for operation. One night near the end of that month Latrobe and a few friends built fires under the boilers of the steam pumps, and the next morning the citizens of Philadelphia were delighted to find pure water gushing out of the new hydrants. Not only did Latrobe's scheme work admirably, but the pumphouse he designed for Centre Square, the heart of the system, possessed a grace far transcending its mundane function; a domed structure of classic proportions, it immensely pleased the citizenry and was a beloved landmark for many years.

Meanwhile other facets of Latrobe's career were developing just as favorably. Construction of the Bank of Pennsylvania went steadily ahead, and by widespread agreement it took shape as the most beautiful large building in Philadelphia—if not in the entire country. It was the first full embodiment of the Greek Revival in America, and the noble simplicity of its lofty Ionic marble columns and superbly vaulted ceilings set an example which had a profound effect on the future of American architecture.

Swiftly becoming known and admired as the man

At Yorktown, Virginia, in 1797, Latrobe found Lord Corn-wallis' former headquarters badly "shattered by shells & balls."

responsible for the new waterworks and the new bank, Latrobe also found in Philadelphia a human relationship which he had been deprived of since his days in England. Mary Elizabeth Hazlehurst, daughter of a prominent merchant, struck him as combining the attributes of beauty, good breeding, wit, and personal warmth that would make him happy; and since the lady was more than willing, they were married in May of 1800. The architect's two young children, whom he had sorely missed since leaving them in England five years before, now arrived, and Latrobe's happiness was complete.

Yet there were irksome problems. As a professional man he depended for his livelihood on fees that came in much less regularly than those of a doctor or lawyer; and there was fiercer competition. In 1802 he submitted an interesting design for the New York City Hall. An influential New York friend, Aaron Burr, predicted an easy win, but the award went to someone else. Latrobe's plans for a stone bridge from Manhattan to Long Island were also rejected: his estimated cost of $950,000 was considered impossibly high. He rebuilt the interior of Nassau Hall, Princeton, after a fire, and designed a handsome building for Dickinson College, in Carlisle, Pennsylvania, which serves to this day; but for both of these educational efforts Latrobe high-mindedly refused any commission. A much bigger assignment, again without pay, was the Roman Catholic Cathedral in Baltimore, which was to keep him busy intermittently for more than a decade. There were other jobs, such as private houses; but the going was so rough that when, in 1802, President Jefferson called him to Washington for consultation on various federal projects, Latrobe felt relieved as well as flattered.

The first assignment Jefferson had in mind for Latrobe was the President's own invention, and one of which he was very fond. Concerned about maintaining the United States Navy ready for action even in peaceful times, he had conceived of an enormous dry dock capable of preserving a dozen frigates under one roof. The grand sweep of the scheme excited Latrobe. He produced, in record time, a preliminary design that even inflated Jefferson's dream: the covered dry dock was to be 165 feet wide and 800 feet long—about the size of a modern dirigible hangar. Expense was estimated at $417,276. The President was greatly pleased, but this was thinking too big for the Congress of 1802. They voted the project down after sarcastic speeches denouncing its Brobdingnagian dimensions and astronomical cost.

The dry-dock scheme at any rate drew Latrobe and Jefferson closely together, and despite inevitable frictions between two men equally strong-minded, they remained good friends. Jefferson was most anxious to get on with the construction of the federal buildings, especially the Capitol, and in the spring of 1803 he appointed Latrobe Surveyor of the Public Buildings of the United States. Now began ten years of intense work that would bring a strange mélange of triumphs, frustrations, satisfactions, and defeats. Latrobe was unwavering in his determination to build a capitol worthy of his own soaring conception of the American destiny; and this he largely achieved against a long series of heartbreaking obstacles. Minor irritations, like Jefferson's suggestion of wooden columns for the House of Representatives, he handled easily. The almost constant complaints and monetary reluctance of Congress, however, at times made his career in Washington almost unendurable; and worse than that, he was working from the start under the disadvantage of plans left by half-successful predecessors.

The chief villain of the piece, from Latrobe's point of view, was Dr. William Thornton, the accomplished dilettante whose basic plans for the Capitol had won George Washington's approval in 1793. Latrobe would have been among the first to acknowledge Thornton as a gifted amateur—but he also understood perhaps better than anyone that the design of such a building was not the province of the amateur. Three architects—Stephen Hallet, George Hadfield, and James Hoban—already had worked under Thornton's supervision, without successfully translating his plans into reality. Now the Doctor was convinced that the newcomer was a usurper out to rob him of his reputation and ruin his design for the Capitol. Latrobe's earnest attempts to explain just what he found wrong in Thornton's plans met with indignant rebuffs. The trouble went far beyond the level of personalities, moreover, for Latrobe found it impossible to correlate precisely the few drawings he was able to get from Thornton with the work actually done on the unfinished south wing—everything was in a state of uncertainty. Still, Congress reverently insisted that "General Washington's" plans —that is, Thornton's—must be adhered to as closely as possible, and Jefferson, although he recognized Latrobe's difficulties, felt obliged to proceed generally on that basis.

In these awkward circumstances Latrobe's usually civil temper was put under strain, yet in the early stages of the controversy he was able to joke about his troubles with Thornton. One problem was the shape of the House chamber. Thornton's plan called for a great oval, and some of the foundations were laid with that in view. Latrobe, convinced that such a chamber would have grave deficiencies of lighting and acoustics, would have preferred a single semicircle; but he went ahead in accordance with Jefferson's wishes, merely modifying the oval into two semicircles connected in the center by a rectangular space. "Of this I can make a *very good thing of the sort*," he wrote his chief assistant, explaining the italics with an anecdote about an old gentleman named Izzard, who was asked whether so-and-so was not "a good sort of man." "'N, N, Ne-ne-no!' said Mr. Izzard, who stuttered violently, 'He, he, he's a goo-good man of a G, G God damn'd bad sort.' This I say of my plan and no more."

With all his troubles, the calendar of Latrobe's Washington years—he moved his family there in 1807 and they stayed until 1813—marked many days of pleasure and excitement. The new federal capital was a bustling place. It was raw and unfinished, a "city of magnificent distances" as one foreign visitor called it, but it was the heart of the youthful country's national activity, and it pulsed with a sense of the future. In the new houses that went up at a brisk and fairly steady rate, a broad variety of social entertainments spun themselves into an exhilarating social whirl. Mary Latrobe, the architect's wife, had been a childhood friend of Dolley Madison in Philadelphia, and with such an entree the Latrobes themselves were soon the center of an active and brilliant group. In addition to the Madisons and the Jeffersons, they visited or were visited by the Joel Barlows, the Bushrod Washingtons, the Henry Clays, Robert Fulton, Washington Irving, Gilbert Stuart, and scores of others whose names are far less familiar but whose social attributes were no less delightful. Meanwhile Latrobe's own name gradually assumed national prominence, his days were full of hard but rewarding work, and his charming children—there were now five—grew older and more accomplished.

Like most parents, however, the Latrobes occasion-

ally had reason to doubt the wisdom of their offspring. In 1805 the oldest girl, Lydia, had stunned them by falling precipitately in love, at the age of thirteen, with Nicholas Roosevelt of New York and New Jersey, a great-great-uncle of "T. R." One of the leading industrial entrepreneurs of the period, Roosevelt had built the big steam engines for the Philadelphia waterworks, and was among Latrobe's closest friends. He ardently returned Lydia's passion, and despite their daughter's tender age the Latrobes might have looked upon the lovers with some benevolence except for one thing. Nicholas Roosevelt at thirty-seven was less than four years younger than Latrobe himself, and thus literally old enough to be Lydia's father. The thing was impossible, the Latrobes felt, and they made almost desperate efforts to discourage it.

Their attempts were strikingly unsuccessful. Roosevelt and Lydia had become so violently enamoured that nothing short of stark prohibition would have deflected them; and Latrobe, who loved them both, was not much inclined to prohibit. He did demand a year's "probation," hoping that the relationship might cool, but they broke it with secret letters and even secret meetings. Then a lovers' quarrel did occur, and for more than a year it looked as if the whole thing was indeed over. But Roosevelt was a houseguest not long after the Latrobes moved to Washington, and immediately the attachment was fervently resumed. By this time both Latrobe and his wife were reconciled—Lydia had become, at seventeen, one of Washington's most attractive young ladies—and the marriage took place in the autumn of 1808. Dispelling all the fears of the parents, it turned out to be not only happy but full of excitement. One highlight was the fantastic maiden voyage of the *New Orleans,* first steamboat on the Mississippi, which Roosevelt built for Robert Fulton (see Leonard V. Huber's "Heyday of the Floating Palace," in the October, 1957, AMERICAN HERITAGE). Lydia was on that voyage, twenty years old, pregnant and scared, but dauntlessly pleased to share her husband's historic adventure.

By the time the War of 1812 hovered on the political horizon, Benjamin Latrobe had finished a major contribution to the architecture of the United States Capitol. Under his direction the south wing was carried to completion as the most beautiful legislative chamber in the Western world. The design was Latrobe's not only architecturally, but in terms of interior decoration, for he had specified most of the sculpture, the great crimson draperies, and the furniture. He also carried out, against formidable obstacles, a thorough renovation of Thornton's defective work in

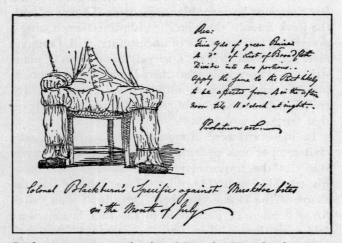

Back-country customs intrigued Latrobe. Here he shows one method of adapting knee breeches to frustrate "muskitoes."

the north wing. As an additional task, Latrobe undertook the extensive work of redecorating the White
House in keeping with Dolley Madison's perceptive
taste, when the new administration began in 1809.

But the war was to leave most of his work in ruins.
Not only did the British burn the White House in
1814, but the Capitol, too, was put to the torch, and
its interiors thoroughly gutted. According to a story
repeated by John H. B. Latrobe, the architect's son,
the British officer assigned to burn the Hall of Representatives paused in the entrance, and declared that
it was a pity to burn anything so beautiful.

It was a time of multiple distress for Latrobe. The
product of thousands of hours of devoted labor went
up in smoke, and his financial affairs, never really
prosperous, had recently taken the worst turn in years.
For all his professional acumen Latrobe was a poor
businessman, and time and again private ventures—
several of them in connection with Nicholas Roosevelt—ended in minor disaster. On top of that he was
an easy touch for any friend wanting to borrow money,
and by 1813 Latrobe had decided that to remain longer
in Washington would mean bankruptcy. The most
hopeful prospect for reviving his fortune seemed to
be the steamboat business, in which both his son-in-
law and his friend Robert Fulton were heavily engaged. Fulton had set up a company to navigate the
Ohio River by steam, and Latrobe arranged to move
to Pittsburgh to superintend the construction of some
of the boats. He left Washington in a bitter mood,
writing to a friend that he was "bidding an eternal
adieu to . . . this community . . . the more you stir
it, the more it stinketh."

He found Pittsburgh not much better, although at
first the evils seemed merely physical: "Whoever can
make up his mind to breathe dirt, & eat dirt, & be up
to his knees in dirt," Latrobe told a correspondent,
"may live very happily & comfortably here." Unfortunately it was not that simple. An account of his
enterprises in Pittsburgh would be a tedious tale of
further business failure, for zooming construction
costs, rough competition, and serious misunderstand-
ings with Fulton soon brought the steamboat company
to absolute collapse. With it Latrobe's health also collapsed. He had reached the bottom of his luck, and
his letters in the spring of 1815 reveal a man sick in
mind and body and almost at the point of giving up.

It was his brave wife Mary who saved him in this
crisis. Without her husband's knowledge she wrote
eloquent and persuasive letters to the James Madisons
and to her other important Washington friends, urging that Latrobe's talents be used in rebuilding the
ruined United States Capitol. She was rewarded with
a large envelope carrying the President's seal and con-

*"Temperance, Temperance, I say, & so says St. Paul," was the
exhortation of this preacher at a revival meeting in 1809.*

taining an offer to reappoint Latrobe as the Capitol
architect. He "wept like a child" when she presented
it to him.

By July of 1815 they were back in Washington, with
Latrobe surveying the rubble left by the British and
already turning out dozens of drawings for the reconstruction. The south wing had been so fully demolished that he was able to redesign the House chamber
in the shape he had always thought it should have—
one large semicircle; and in many other matters the
havoc of the British gave Latrobe scope for imagina-
tive improvements. It was at this time that he designed
his famous "tobacco capitals" for the columns of the
Senate rotunda—still a tourist attraction, as are the
"corn-cob capitals" he had done earlier for the Senate
vestibule, which had survived the burning.

Yet his old troubles soon returned to vex him anew,
this time aggravated by the fact that President James
Monroe, who took office in 1817, gradually became
convinced that Latrobe was extravagant with public
money and slow to achieve results because of over-
attention to his private interests. These questionable
conclusions were actively promoted by Colonel Samuel
Lane, the official intermediary between Latrobe and
Monroe. Under pressure from Congress to find a scape-
goat for the inevitable building delays, and with a
dictatorial personality naturally negative to Latrobe's,
Lane soon became his sworn enemy.

To Latrobe's professional frustrations personal anguish was now added. His talented son Henry had
gone to New Orleans to act as his father's agent in the
design and construction of a water system which, it
was hoped, might rid the city of yellow fever. The
young man had done extremely well in advancing the
project; but in September, 1817, he suddenly fell sick
and died, a victim of the disease he had dreamed of

defeating. It was all too much to bear, and in November, 1817, Latrobe submitted his resignation. He did it with dignity, and he saw to it that Monroe received a full set of drawings so that his successor—who turned out to be Charles Bulfinch—could profit by them in finishing the work on the Capitol. Once more Latrobe left Washington under a pall, his prospects darkly in doubt; and this time he filed legal notice of bankruptcy.

There followed a quiet interval in Baltimore, where he had been engaged since 1816 to design, in partnership with Maximilian Godefroy, a mercantile exchange— a big, airy building which was not torn down until 1901. This brought in some cash for current expenses; and he also had the satisfaction of seeing his great cathedral rise to three-dimensional beauty. But his best work was now behind him. He suffered the humiliation, in 1818, of taking second place in a competition for the design of a new Bank of the United States, the award going ironically to William Strickland, who had received much of his training as an apprentice under Latrobe.

Nothing else in the East looked promising, and meanwhile construction of the New Orleans waterworks was languishing. There were two remaining sons, both so gifted that they would one day be well-known in their own right, but too young to help in 1818. (The older, John H. B. Latrobe, became a renowned lawyer; the younger, Benjamin Henry, Jr., took up civil engineering with conspicuous success.) There seemed no solution short of parting from his family for a while, and in December, 1818, Latrobe set sail for New Orleans on a brig suggestively named the *Clio*. For he was now entering upon the last chapter of his personal history.

The sea voyage and the following months in New Orleans were tonic to the tired architect. He had time on his hands and a new environment to explore, much as during his earliest days in America in 1796. Again he took up his journals and his beloved water coloring, recording the sights and sounds of French New Orleans in eager detail. He found much to fascinate him and partially heal the grief over his lost son—a civilization different enough from that of the eastern seaboard to bring out all his curiosity and his shrewd, always humane reactions. He loved the native market place, and wandered there making sketches. The beauty of the Creole ladies at a Washington's Birthday ball dazzled him, but he had recently witnessed, at his boardinghouse, a savage beating administered by the landlady to a Negro girl whom Latrobe had come to consider a paragon among servants; and he knew of other such incidents. This seriously dampened his pleasure at the ball: "I fancied that I saw a cowskin in every pretty hand gracefully waved in the dance." He went to the theatre; he watched the Negroes in their Sunday amusements of singing and dancing; he committed to his journal long thoughts on religion engendered by a comparison of Catholicism and Protestantism as represented in New Orleans—coming out himself, as a true child of the Enlightenment, in favor of a natural religion "unprofaned by external dictation."

But Latrobe's respite from trouble was not to be long. By the summer of 1819 he was very hard at work on the water system, and encountering typical hindrances. Courageously he struggled over each in turn, and in September felt far enough ahead to go North and bring back his wife and two young children. The spring and summer of 1820 found him well established in New Orleans, with enough commissions (besides the waterworks) to bring both hope of financial success at last, and a firm professional reputation in the city. Despite a yellow fever epidemic in the late summer, Latrobe personally superintended the digging of a ditch for the main suction pipe of the water system, ignoring the armadas of mosquitoes that hummed by the riverbank. On September 3, just three years after the death of his son, he fell sick with yellow fever, took to his bed, and died a few hours later.

Latrobe himself left what is perhaps his most appropriate epitaph. In those twilight months in New Orleans, looking back over his busy and harried career, he remembered the happy days in Philadelphia when his new marriage and his success with the Bank of Pennsylvania seemed to augur a future of glory. An incident came to his mind that struck him, among a thousand, as having given him more "particular satisfaction" than any other in his life, and he set it down in his journal:

Walking up Second Street [where the Bank was situated] I observed two French officers standing opposite the building and looking at it without saying a word. I stepped into Black's shop and stood close to them. After some time one of them exclaimed several times, *"C'est si beau, et si simple!"* He said no more and stood for a few minutes longer before he walked away with his companion.

Paul F. Norton, a specialist in the history of architecture, has taught at Pennsylvania State University, and is now chairman of the Department of Art at the University of Massachusetts. In doing research for this article and for the captions in the accompanying portfolio, he made a special study of the Latrobe collection at the Maryland Historical Society, Baltimore. Mr. Halliday, formerly a professor at North Carolina State College, recently joined our staff.

For further reading: Benjamin Henry Latrobe, *by Talbot Hamlin (Oxford University Press, 1955).*

A Latrobe Portfolio

Benjamin Henry Latrobe left to future generations a colorful and graphic record of America between 1795, when he sailed from England on an American ship, and 1820, when he died in New Orleans. From the fine collection gathered by the Maryland Historical Society, AMERICAN HERITAGE is privileged to present a wide selection, chosen to suggest the range of the architect's interests and accomplishments, as well as the highlights of his career. Many of the color illustrations are here published for the first time. On his fifteen-week voyage to America, Latrobe amused himself with such intricate whimsies as the trompe l'oeil *pictured above. Amid sardonic souvenirs of rough weather and shipboard ennui, he included a meticulously realistic sketch-within-a-sketch, showing the ship's dining table ready to serve its nine cabin passengers. His description mentions "a basket of Biscuit, all alive-o!" and the "slop bason" which "also . . . serves to wash Mrs. Taylor's baby." The water color below shows how the* Eliza, *a vessel of 286 tons, might have looked from another ship while bucking an Atlantic storm.*

First Impressions

During his first two years in America, Latrobe filled his sketchbooks with drawings and water colors that give a unique impression of how the country looked to an inquiring eye in his time. While he chose his subjects with sharp aesthetic sensibility, the interests of the geographer, historian, and engineer are also evident. The view of Norfolk, at left, he annotated precisely, using a system of co-ordinates to indicate particular points of interest. "Norfolk is an illbuilt, unhealthy town," he wrote. "The house on the point CC [center of picture] is the Custom house, a mean timber building. The Main Street runs up between that & the next house to the right." River navigation, so important to a young nation of primitive roads, absorbed much of his technical concern, and he made several journeys along the Appomattox and the Potomac to survey the possibilities of improvement by dredging. The scene above is identified, in Latrobe's sketchbook, as "the Bridge at the little Falls of the Potowmac about 3 miles above Georgetown. The span of the Bridge is about 120 feet. . . . It was framed in New England of White pine, & brought hither by Water."

Journeying up the Appomattox in the summer of 1796, Latrobe stopped occasionally to paint a scene that struck his fancy. Explaining the picture at right, he noted: ". . . we walked up the hill to Mr. Walk's house, where we were determined to stay all night; no introduction or previous notice being necessary in this hospitable country. . . . The morning of June the 15th was chiefly employed in strolling about. I took a view of Mr. Walk's mill on Flat creek, a wretched . . . mill in a most advantageous situation." A few weeks earlier he had visited Williamsburg, Virginia, already in need of restoration less than twenty years after its desertion as state capital in 1779: "Many ruined & uninhabited houses disgrace the streets." In the former capitol building, he made a drawing of "a beautiful statue of Lord Bottetourt, a popular governor of Virginia before the war . . . deprived of its head and mutilated in many other respects." Latrobe's careful sketch and his notes were useful in returning the statue to something like its original state during the modern restoration of Williamsburg. The College of William and Mary will place it in its projected new library there.

Sketch of Mr Walke Mill on Flat Creek, near its junction with Appomattox river.

Wedding Journey

On their honeymoon in May, 1800, Latrobe and his bride went from Philadelphia to New York. They stopped en route to visit relatives, as well as Latrobe's friend and future son-in-law, Nicholas Roosevelt, who lived at Newark, New Jersey. They also made detours for the sake of scenery. Where a modern bridegroom might take snapshots, Latrobe paused to make sketches or water colors. Above, he achieved a fine vista along the road—evidently one of America's first divided highways—from Newark to Paterson. "This view," he remarked in his sketchbook, "shows the Gap in the Mountains through which the Passaick finds its way to the Ocean." The falls of the Passaic, which fascinated the artist by their geological formations as well as their great beauty, are shown at right; the quick pen-and-ink sketches below carry Latrobe's own captions.

My cousin enjoying the country air on the Frankfort road

Washington tavern.
Cyder? no, damn Cyder! I can give you
good spirits!

Endurance and Change

Small trace of present-day Richmond can be seen in Latrobe's 1796 painting, above. Even the state capitol, designed by Jefferson in admiring imitation of the Roman temple at Nîmes, has been much transformed; and the other architectural features of the landscape it once dominated have been swept away. On the other hand, Latrobe's view of the Hudson Palisades might be fresh from a modern painter's brush except for the masts rising from a ship on the river.

On one of several business trips to Lancaster, Pennsylvania, in the first years of the nineteenth century, Latrobe made this fine colored drawing of the courthouse, then the state capitol (above). That he never got beyond sketching in the human figures suggests the busy pace of his life at this time. Yet he did take the occasion to visit the legislative chamber, noting in a letter to his wife that among the representatives, "I counted only twelve combed heads and two woolen nightcaps." Heads, nightcaps, and the building itself are gone; but here and there in Pennsylvania can still be found examples of the type of massive stone barn, German-American in style, that Latrobe pictured in the water color below.

"An overseer doing his duty" (Fredericksburg)

"Preparation for the enjoyment of a fine Sunday"

"Richmond: Sketch in the Court of Appeals"

"Market folks" (New Orleans, 1819)

Sketches from
Everyday Life

A Conversation at See   *March 10th 1797*

The common life of the young country interested Latrobe, and he often caught its flavor in quick sketches, satiric, comic, or merely colorful. The titles of those opposite are self-explanatory. "A Conversation at Sea," above, (evidently made on a coastal voyage) is supplied by Latrobe with this dialogue:

QUESTION: Hooooooagh. . . ANSWER: Noooooooagh. . .

QUESTION: Whence came ye? ANSWER: From Stoningtown.

QUESTION: Where's that? ANSWER: You're a fine fellow for a Captain not to know where
Stoningtown is.

QUESTION: (Aside: Damn your Yankee Soul.) Where are you bound? ANSWER: To Savannah, if ye know where that is.

QUESTION: What have you in? ANSWER: Only a few Notions.

QUESTION: What's your Longitude? ANSWER: Right enough. Zebadiah make sail, up helm!

49

Public Monuments

Latrobe's principal fame rests on his pioneer work as an architect. Bringing professional skill and standards from his training abroad, he profoundly shaped this country's architecture not only in his own work, but in his influence on younger men. A leader in the classical revival, he was solidly supported by Thomas Jefferson, during whose two terms as President (1801-09) Latrobe accomplished a major part of his work on the United States Capitol. (The pencil sketch of Jefferson, left, has been authoritatively attributed to the architect.) Below is a drawing for the west elevation of the Capitol as Latrobe planned it; actually most of the middle section was done after he left Washington, by Charles Bulfinch. Latrobe had envisaged a low dome, as shown; Bulfinch built a higher one which in turn was replaced, during the Civil War, by the very high dome (designed by Thomas U. Walter) that greets visitors to Washington today. Although the famous porticoes of the White House were not built until after the architect's death, they carried out the designs Latrobe had made during James Madison's administration. His drawing for the south portico is shown at left center. Latrobe also found time to serve as interior decorator for "the President's House," and, according to Dolley Madison, "Mr. Latrobe's elegant taste [was] justly admired." The sketches for the Centre Square pump house of the Philadelphia waterworks (below, left) demonstrate Latrobe's conviction that there need be no divorce between efficiency and aesthetic appeal.

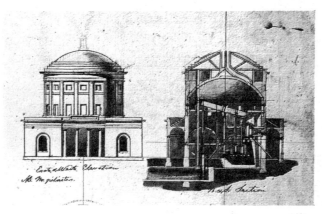

Above: The first Roman Catholic cathedral in the United States stands today in Baltimore much as it looks in Latrobe's drawing, made sometime during his years of intermittent work on it from 1804 to 1818. Below: In 1815 the architect surveyed the havoc done to the Capitol by the War of 1812, and made this annotated sketch showing how close the columns of the Hall of Representatives came to collapsing.

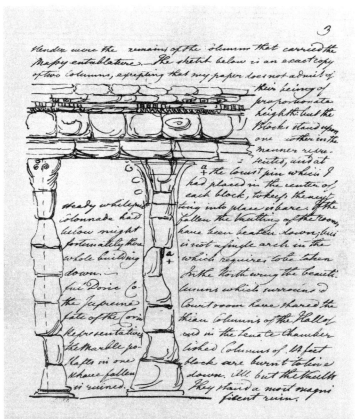

Dreams Unfulfilled

Some of Latrobe's fondest architectural schemes failed, either through lack of funds or, occasionally, because a rival defeated him in competition for a commission. His design for the New York City Hall (below, right) was, he thought, one of his best; but the award went to the more lavish plans of Mangin and McComb. Their building, which Latrobe sourly called "a vile heterogeneous composition," is still a New York landmark. Latrobe's city hall would have been a simpler structure, almost austerely economical, but lacking something in grandeur for the chief building of a great metropolis. His plans for the Baltimore Library, right, were accepted with satisfaction by the group concerned, but raising enough money to carry them out proved to be another matter. Similarly, the fine combination hotel and theatre (below, left), which Latrobe designed for Richmond, went hopelessly beyond the cold realities of cash.

Latrobe's elegant perspective drawing of the ballroom and his sectional view of the hotel chambers and the theatre itself both suggest that in not realizing his design Richmond lost a theatrical center far advanced for its time.

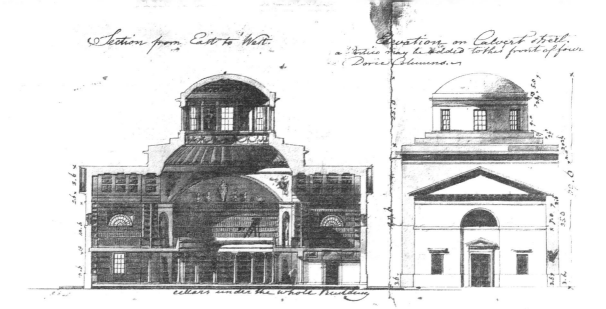

Section from East to West.

Elevation on Calvert Street.
a Portico may be added to the front of four
Doric Columns.

cellars under the whole Building

Latrobe's Favorite

Of all his architectural designs that were actually translated into stone, Latrobe's favorite was the Bank of Pennsylvania, completed in Philadelphia in 1800. It was his first great Amer-

ican success; it was the first full American embodiment of the Greek Revival; and it was a product of perhaps the happiest period of his life. It survived until after the Civil War, when it was torn down to make room for a government building of no particular distinction. Latrobe's drawing reveals, as art historian Fiske Kimball once wrote, "what posterity has lost."

View of the Balize, at the mouth of the Mississippi. A the Spanish look out. B, a lookout lately built. The U.S. Schooner Firebrand in the Bayou. The Custom boat, formerly Mitchell the pirate's. Jan. 7, 1819

End of the Journey

In New Orleans early in 1819, Latrobe again took up his pleasant hobby of painting water colors. His captions for this pair, shown just as they appear in his sketchbook, suggest the keen and steady curiosity that typified the architect from the start of his American life in 1796 to its tragic end in 1820.

View from the window of my Chamber at Tremoulet's hotel New Orleans. The distant houses are in the suburb St. Mary. The house of which the roof occupies the center of the view is the Government house. The opening beyond the flat roof in the foreground is Jefferson street.

By ALAN F. WESTIN

Ride-in!

It began one day early in January when a Negro named Robert Fox boarded a streetcar in Louisville, Kentucky, dropped his coin into the fare box, and sat down in the white section of the car. Ordered to move, he refused, and the driver threw him off the car. Shortly after, Fox filed a charge of assault and battery against the streetcar company in the federal district court, claiming that separate seating policies were illegal and the driver's actions were therefore improper. The district judge instructed the jury that under federal law common carriers must serve all passengers equally without regard to race. So instructed, the jury found the company rules to be invalid and awarded damages of fifteen dollars (plus $72.80 in legal costs) to Mr. Fox.

Immediately there was sharp criticism of the Fox decision from the city and state administrations, both Democratic; the company defied the court's ruling and continued segregated seating. After several meetings with local federal officials and white attorneys co-operating with them, Louisville Negro leaders decided to launch a full-scale "ride-in." At 7 P.M. on May 12, a young Negro boy boarded a streetcar near the Willard Hotel, walked past the driver, and took a seat among the white passengers. The driver, under new company regulations, did not attempt to throw him off but simply stopped the car, lit a cigar, and refused to proceed until the Negro moved to "his place." While the governor, the Louisville chief of police, and other prominent citizens looked on from the sidewalks, a large crowd which included an increasingly noisy mob of jeering white teen-agers gathered around the streetcar.

Before long, there were shouts of "Put him out!" "Hit him!" "Kick him!" "Hang him!" Several white youths climbed into the car and began yelling insults in the face of the young Negro rider. He refused to answer—or to move. The youths dragged him from his seat, pulled him off the car, and began to beat him. Only when the Negro started to defend himself did the city police intervene: they arrested him for disturbing the peace and took him to jail.

This time the trial was held in Louisville city court, not the federal court. The magistrate ruled that streetcar companies were not under any obligation to treat Negroes exactly as they treated whites, and that any federal measures purporting to create such obligations would be "clearly invalid" under the constitutions of Kentucky and the United States. The defendant was fined, and the judge delivered a warning to Louisville Negroes that further ride-ins would be punished.

But the ride-in campaign was not halted that easily. In the following days, streetcar after streetcar was entered by Negroes who took seats in the white section. Now the drivers got off the cars entirely. On several occasions, the Negro riders drove the cars themselves, to the sound of cheers from Negro spectators. Then violence erupted. Bands of white youths and men began to throw Negro riders off the cars; windows were broken, cars were overturned, and for a time a general race riot threatened. Moderate Kentucky newspapers

THOMAS NAST

Ride-ins and sit-ins are not new tactics of the Negro.
They were first tried back in the 1870's, and with great success.
But that time High Court decisions were very different

and many community leaders deplored the fighting; the Republican candidate for governor denounced the streetcar company's segregation policies and blamed the violence on Democratic encouragement of white extremists.

By this time, newspapers across the country were carrying reports of the conflict, and many editorials denounced the seating regulations. In Louisville, federal marshals and the United States attorney backed the rights of the Negro riders and stated that federal court action would be taken if necessary. There were even rumors that the President might send troops.

Under these threats, the streetcar company capitulated. Soon, all the city transit companies declared that "it was useless to try to resist or evade the enforcement by the United States authorities of the claim of Negroes to ride in the cars." To "avoid serious collisions," the company would thereafter allow all passengers to sit where they chose. Although a few disturbances took place in the following months, and some white intransigents boycotted the streetcars, mixed seating became a common practice. The Kentucky press soon pointed with pride to the spirit of conciliation and harmony which prevailed in travel facilities within the city, calling it a model for good race relations. Never again would Louisville streetcars be segregated.

The event may have the familiar ring of recent history, but it is not, for it occurred ninety-one years ago, in 1871. The streetcars were horse-drawn. The President who considered ordering troops to Louisville was ex-General Grant, not ex-General Eisenhower. The Republican gubernatorial candidate who supported the Negro riders, John Marshall Harlan, was not a post-World War II leader of the G.O.P. but a former slaveholder from one of Kentucky's oldest and most famous political families. And the "new" Negroes who waged this ride-in were not members of the Congress of Racial Equality and the National Association for the Advancement of Colored People, or followers of Dr. Martin Luther King, but former slaves who were fighting for civil rights in their own time, and with widespread success.

And yet these dramatic sit-ins, ride-ins, and walk-ins of the 1870's are almost unknown to the American public today. The standard American histories do not mention them, providing only thumbnail references to "bayonet-enforced" racial contacts during Reconstruction. Most commentators view the Negro's resort to direct action as an invention of the last decade. Clearly, then, it is time that the civil-rights struggle of the 1870's and 1880's was rescued from newspaper files and court archives, not only because it is historically important but also because it has compelling relevance for our own era.

Contrary to common assumptions today, no state in the Union during the 1870's, including those south of the Mason-Dixon line, required separation of whites and Negroes in places of public accommodation. Admission and arrangement policies were up to individual owners. In the North and West, many theatres, hotels, restaurants, and public carriers served Negro patrons without hesitation or discrimination. Some accepted Negroes only in second-class accommodations, such as smoking cars on railroads or balconies in theatres, where they sat among whites who did not have first-class tickets. Other northern and western establishments, especially the more exclusive ones, refused Negro patronage entirely.

The situation was similar in the larger cities of the southern and border states. Many establishments admitted Negroes to second-class facilities. Some gave first-class service to those of privileged social status—government officials, army officers, newspapermen, and clergymen. On the other hand, many places of public accommodation, particularly in the rural areas and smaller cities of the South, were closed to Negroes whatever their wealth or status.

From 1865 through the early 1880's, the general trend in the nation was toward wider acceptance of Negro patronage. The federal Civil Rights Act of 1866, with its guarantee to Negroes of "equal benefit of the laws," had set off a flurry of enforcement suits—for denying berths to Negroes on a Washington-New York train; for refusing to sell theatre tickets to Negroes in Boston; and for barring Negro women from the waiting rooms and parlor cars of railroads in Virginia, Illinois, and California. Ratification of the Fourteenth Amendment in 1868 had spurred more challenges. Three northern states, and two southern states under

Reconstruction regimes, passed laws making it a crime for owners of public-accommodation businesses to discriminate. Most state and federal court rulings on these laws between 1865 and 1880 held in favor of Negro rights, and the rulings built up a steady pressure on owners to relax racial bars.

Nevertheless, instances of exclusion and segregation continued throughout the 1870's. To settle the issue once and for all (thereby reaping the lasting appreciation of the Negro voters), congressional Republicans led by Senator Charles Sumner pressed for a federal statute making discrimination in public accommodations a crime. Democrats and conservative Republicans warned in the congressional debates that such a law would trespass on the reserved powers of the states and reminded the Sumner supporters that recent Supreme Court decisions had taken a narrow view of federal power under the Civil War amendments.

After a series of legislative compromises, however, Sumner's forces were able to enact the statute; on March 1, 1875, "An Act to Protect all Citizens in their Civil and Legal Rights" went into effect. "It is essential to just government," the preamble stated, that the nation "recognize the equality of all men before the law, and . . . it is the duty of government in its dealings with the people to mete out equal and exact justice to all, of whatever nativity, race, color, or persuasion, religious or political . . ."

Section 1 of the act declared that "All persons within the jurisdiction of the United States shall be entitled to the full and equal enjoyment of the accommodations . . . of inns, public conveyances on land or water, theaters and other places of public amusement; subject only to the conditions and limitations established by law, and applicable alike to citizens of every race or color. . . ." Section 2 provided that any person

This etching of the Supreme Court in session (below) was made soon after its far-reaching civil-rights decision of 1883.

violating the act could be sued in federal district court for a penalty of $500, could be fined $500 to $1,000, or could be imprisoned from thirty days to one year. (A separate section forbade racial discrimination in the selection of juries.)

Reaction to the law was swift. Two Negro men were admitted to the dress circle of Macauley's Theatre in Louisville and sat through the performance without incident. In Washington, Negroes were served for the first time at the bar of the Willard Hotel, and a Negro broke the color line when he was seated at McVicker's Theatre in Chicago. But in other instances, Negroes were rejected despite "Sumner's law." Several hotels in Chattanooga turned in their licenses, became private boardinghouses, and accepted whites only. Restaurants and barber shops in Richmond turned away Negro customers.

Suits challenging refusals were filed en masse throughout the country. Perhaps a hundred were decided in the federal district courts during the late 1870's and early 1880's. Federal judges in Pennsylvania, Texas, Maryland, and Kentucky, among others, held the law to be constitutional and ruled in favor of Negro complainants. In North Carolina, New Jersey, and California, however, district judges held the law invalid. And when other courts in New York, Tennessee, Missouri, and Kansas put the issue to the federal circuit judges, the judges divided on the question, and the matter was certified to the United States Supreme Court.

But the Supreme Court did not exactly rush to make its ruling. Though two cases testing the 1875 act reached it in 1876 and a third in 1877, the Justices simply held them on their docket. In 1879, the Attorney General filed a brief defending the constitutionality of the law, but still the Court reached no decisions. In 1880, three additional cases were filed, but two years elapsed before the Solicitor General presented a fresh

brief supporting the statute. It was not until late in 1883 that the Supreme Court passed upon the 1875 act, in what became famous as the *Civil Rights Cases* ruling. True, the Court was badly behind in its work in this period, but clearly the Justices chose to let the civil-rights cases "ripen" for almost eight years.

When they finally came to grips with the issue, six separate test suits were involved. The most celebrated had arisen in New York City in November of 1879. Edwin Booth, the famous tragedian and brother of John Wilkes Booth, had opened a special Thanksgiving week engagement at the Grand Opera House. After playing *Hamlet, Othello,* and *Richelieu* to packed houses, he was scheduled to perform Victor Hugo's *Ruy Blas* at the Saturday matinee on November 22.

One person who had decided to see Booth that Saturday was William R. Davis, Jr., who was later described in the press as a tall, handsome, and well-spoken Negro of twenty-six. He was the business agent of the *Progressive-American,* a Negro weekly published in New York City. At 10 o'clock Saturday morning, Davis' girl friend ("a bright octoroon, almost white," as the press put it), purchased two reserved seats at the box office of the Grand Opera House. At 1:30 P.M., Davis and his lady presented themselves at the theatre, only to be told by the doorkeeper, Samuel Singleton, that "these tickets are no good." If he would step out to the box office, Singleton told Davis, his money would be refunded.

It is unlikely that Davis was surprised by Singleton's action, for this was not the first time he had encountered such difficulties. Shortly after the passage of the 1875 act, Davis had been refused a ticket to the dress circle of Booth's Theatre in New York. He had sworn out a warrant against the ticket seller, but the failure of his witnesses to appear at the grand jury proceedings had led to a dismissal of the complaint. This earlier episode, as well as Davis' activity as a Negro journalist, made it probable that this appearance at the Opera House in 1879 was a deliberate test of the management's discriminatory policies.

Though Davis walked out of the lobby at Singleton's request, he did not turn in his tickets for a refund. Instead, he summoned a young white boy standing near the theatre, gave him a dollar (plus a dime for his trouble), and had him purchase two more tickets. When Davis and his companion presented these to Singleton, only the lady was allowed to pass. Again

Justice John Marshall Harlan

Davis was told that his ticket was "no good." When he now refused to move out of the doorway, Singleton called a policeman and asked that Davis be escorted off the theatre property. The officer told Davis that the Messrs. Poole and Donnelly, the managers of the Opera House, did not admit colored persons. "Perhaps the managers do not," Davis retorted, "but the laws of the country [do]."

The following Monday, November 24, Davis filed a criminal complaint; on December 9, this time with witnesses in abundance, Singleton was indicted in what the press described as the first criminal proceeding under the 1875 act to go to trial in New York. When the case opened on January 14, 1880, Singleton's counsel argued that the 1875 law was unconstitutional. "It interferes," he said, "with the right of the State of New York to provide the means under which citizens of the State have the power to control and protect their rights in respect to their private property." The assistant United States attorney replied that such a conception of states' rights had been "exploded and superseded long ago." It was unthinkable, he declared, that "the United States could not extend to one citizen of New York a right which the State itself gave to others of its citizens—the right of admission to places of public amusement."

The presiding judge decided to take the constitutional challenge under advisement and referred it to the circuit court, for consideration at its February term. This left the decision up to Justice Samuel Blatchford of the Supreme Court, who was assigned to the circuit court for New York, and District Judge William Choate. The two judges reached opposite conclusions and certified the question to the United States Supreme Court.

Davis' case, under the title of *United States v. Singleton,* reached the Supreme Court in 1880. Already lodged on the Court's docket were four similar criminal prosecutions under the act of 1875. *U.S. v. Stanley* involved the refusal of Murray Stanley in 1875 to serve a meal at his hotel in Topeka, Kansas, to a Negro, Bird Gee. *U.S. v. Nichols* presented the refusal in 1876 of Samuel Nichols, owner of the Nichols House in Jefferson City, Missouri, to accept a Negro named W. H. R. Agee as a guest. *U.S. v. Ryan* involved the conduct of Michael Ryan, doorkeeper of Maguire's Theatre in San Francisco, in denying a Negro named George M. Tyler entry to the dress circle on January 4, 1876. In *U.S. v. Hamilton,* James Hamilton, a conductor on the Nashville, Chattanooga, and St. Louis Railroad, had on April 21, 1879, denied a Negro woman with a first-class ticket access to the ladies' car.

There was a fifth case, with a somewhat different setting. On the evening of May 22, 1879, Mrs. Sallie J. Robinson, a twenty-eight-year-old Negro, purchased two first-class tickets at Grand Junction, Tennessee, for a trip to Lynchburg, Virginia, on the Memphis and Charleston Railroad. Shortly after midnight she and her nephew, Joseph C. Robinson, described as a young Negro "of light complexion, light hair, and light blue eyes," boarded the train and started into the parlor car. The conductor, C. W. Reagin, held Mrs. Robinson back ("bruising her arm and jerking her roughly around," she alleged) and pushed her into the smoker.

A few minutes later, when Joseph informed the conductor that he was Mrs. Robinson's nephew and was a Negro, the conductor looked surprised. In that case, he said, they could go into the parlor car at the next stop. The Robinsons finished the ride in the parlor car but filed complaints with the railroad about their treatment and then sued for $500 under the 1875 act. At the trial, Reagin testified that he had thought Joseph to be a white man with a colored woman, and his experience was that such associations were "for illicit purposes."

Counsel for the Robinsons objected to Reagin's testimony, on the ground that his actions were based on race and constituted no defense. Admitting the constitutionality of the 1875 law for purposes of the trial, the railroad contended that the action of its conductor did not fall within the statute. The district judge ruled that the motive for excluding persons was the decisive issue under the act: if the jury believed that the conductor had acted because he thought Mrs. Robinson "a prostitute travelling with her paramour," whether "well or ill-founded" in that assumption, the exclusion was not because of race and the railroad was not liable. The jury found for the railroad, and the Robinsons appealed.

These, with William Davis' suit against the doorkeeper of New York's Grand Opera House, were the six cases to which the Supreme Court finally turned in 1882. The Justices were presented with a learned and eloquent brief for the United States submitted by Solicitor General Samuel F. Phillips, who reviewed the leading cases, described the history of the Civil War amendments to the Constitution, and stressed the importance to the rights of citizens of equal access to public accommodation. Four times since 1865, Phillips noted, civil-rights legislation had been enacted by a Congress filled with men who had fought in the Civil War and had written the war amendments. These men understood that "every rootlet of slavery has an indi-

vidual vitality, and, to its minutest hair, should be anxiously followed and plucked up. . . ." They also knew that if the federal government allowed Negroes to be denied accommodation "by persons who notably were sensitive registers of local public opinion," then "what upon yesterday was only 'fact' will become 'doctrine' tomorrow."

The Supreme Court Justices who considered Phillips' brief and the six test cases were uncommonly talented, among them being Chief Justice Morrison R. Waite, a man underrated today; Joseph P. Bradley, that Court's most powerful intellect; and Stephen J. Field, a *laissez-faire* interpreter of American constitutional law. John Marshall Harlan, the youngest man on the Court, had already started on the course which was to mark him as the most frequent and passionate dissenter in the Gilded Age.

As a whole, the Court might have appeared to be one which would have looked favorably on the 1875 Act. All were Republicans except Justice Field, and he was a Democrat appointed by Abraham Lincoln. All except Justice Harlan, who was the Court's only southerner, had made their careers primarily in the northern and western states. Without exception, all had supported the Northern cause in the war, and none had any hostility toward Negroes as a class.

Yet on the afternoon of October 15, 1883, Justice Bradley announced that the Court found Sections 1 and 2 of the Civil Rights Act of 1875 to be unconstitutional. (This disposed of five of the cases; the sixth, *U.S. v. Hamilton*, was denied review on a procedural point.) There was added irony in the fact that Bradley delivered the majority opinion for eight of the Justices. A one-time Whig, Bradley had struggled for a North-South compromise in the darkening months of 1860–61, then had swung to a strong Unionist position after the firing on Fort Sumter. He had run for Congress on the Lincoln ticket in 1862 and in 1868 headed the New Jersey electors for Grant. When the Thirteenth and Fourteenth Amendments were adopted, he had given them firm support, and his appointment to the Supreme Court by Grant in 1870 had drawn no criticism from friends of the Negro, as had the appointment of John Marshall Harlan seven years later.

Bradley's opinion had a tightly reasoned simplicity. The Thirteenth Amendment forbade slavery and involuntary servitude, he noted, but protection against the restoration of bondage could not be stretched to cover federal regulation of "social" discriminations such as those dealt with in the 1875 statute. As for the Fourteenth Amendment, that was addressed only to deprivations of rights by the *states;* it did not encompass *private* acts of discrimination. Thus there was no source of constitutional authority for "Sumner's law"; it had to be regarded as an unwarranted invasion of an area under state jurisdiction. Even as a matter of policy, Bradley argued, the intention of the war amendments to aid the newly freed Negro had to have some limits. At some point, the Negro must cease to be "the special favorite of the law" and take on "the rank of a mere citizen."

At the Atlanta Opera House on the evening of the Court's decision, the end man of Haverly's Minstrels interrupted the performance to announce the ruling. The entire orchestra and dress circle audience rose and cheered. Negroes sitting in the balcony kept their seats, "stunned," according to one newspaper account. A short time earlier, a Negro denied entrance to the dress circle had filed charges against the Opera House management under the 1875 Act. Now his case—their case—was dead.

Of all the nine Justices, only John Marshall Harlan, a Kentuckian and a former slave-holder, announced that he dissented from the ruling. He promised to give a full opinion soon.

Justice Harlan's progress from a supporter of slavery to a civil-rights dissenter makes a fascinating chronicle. Like Bradley, he had entered politics as a Whig and had tried to find a middle road between secessionist Democrats and antislavery Republicans. Like Bradley, he became a Unionist after the firing on Fort Sumter. But there the parallels ended. Although Harlan en-

tered the Union Army, he was totally opposed to freeing the slaves, and his distaste for Lincoln and the Radicals was complete. Between 1863 and 1868, he led the Conservative party in Kentucky, a third-party movement which supported the war but opposed pro-Negro and civil-rights measures as "flagrant invasions of property rights and local government."

By 1868, however, Harlan had become a Republican. The resounding defeat of the Conservatives in the 1867 state elections convinced him that a third party had no future in Kentucky. His antimonopoly views and his general ideas about economic progress conflicted directly with state Democratic policies, and when the Republicans nominated his former field commander, Ulysses S. Grant, for President, in 1868, Harlan was one of the substantial number of Conservatives who joined the G.O.P.

His views on Negro rights also changed at this time. The wave of vigilante activities against white Republicans and Negroes that swept Kentucky in 1868–70, with whippings and murders by the scores, convinced Harlan that federal guarantees were essential. He watched Negroes in Kentucky moving with dignity and skill toward useful citizenship, and his devout Presbyterianism led him to adopt a "brotherhood-of-man" outlook in keeping with his church's national position. Perhaps he may have been influenced by his wife, Mallie, whose parents were New England abolitionists. As a realistic Republican politician, he was also aware that 60,000 Kentucky Negroes would become voters in 1870.

Thus a "new" John Harlan took the stump as Republican gubernatorial candidate in 1871, the year of the Louisville streetcar ride-ins. He opened his rallies by confessing that he had formerly been anti-Negro. But "I have lived long enough," he said, "to feel that the most perfect despotism that ever existed on this earth was the institution of African slavery." The war amendments were necessary "to place it beyond the power of any State to interfere with . . . the results of the war. . . ." The South should stop agitating the race issue, and should turn to rebuilding itself on progressive lines. When the Democrats laughed at "Harlan the Chameleon" and read quotations from his earlier anti-Negro speeches, Harlan replied: "Let it be said that I am right rather than consistent."

Harlan soon became an influential figure in the Republican party and, when President Rutherford B. Hayes decided to appoint a southern Republican to the Supreme Court in 1877, he was a logical choice. Even then, the Negro issue rose to shake Harlan's life again. His confirmation was held up because of doubts by some senators as to his "real" civil-rights views. Only after Harlan produced his speeches between 1871

Harper's Weekly, APRIL 17, 1875

CIVIL RIGHTS. (?)
Waiting for a Five-Hundred-Dollar Kick.

The famous Thomas Nast mocked the provision of the Civil Rights Act of 1875 allowing Negroes to collect $500 from those who barred them from places of public accommodation.

and 1877 and party leaders supported his firmness on the question was he approved.

Once on the Supreme Court, Harlan could have swung back to a conservative position on civil rights. Instead, he became one of his generation's most intense and uncompromising defenders of the Negro. Perhaps his was the psychology of the convert who defends his new faith more passionately, even more combatively, than the born believer. Harlan liked to think that he had changed because he knew the South and realized that any relaxation of federal protection of the rights of Negroes would encourage the "white irreconcilables" first to acts of discrimination and then to violence, which would destroy all hope of accommodation between the races.

When Harlan sat down in October of 1883 to write his dissent in the *Civil Rights Cases,* he hoped to set off a cannon of protest. But he simply could not get his thoughts on paper. He worked late into the night, and even rose from half-sleep to write down ideas that he was afraid would elude him in the morning. "It was a trying time for him," his wife observed. "In point of years, he was much the youngest man on the Bench; and standing alone, as he did in regard to a decision which the whole nation was anxiously awaiting, he felt that . . . he must speak not only forcibly but wisely."

After weeks of drafting and discarding, Harlan seemed to reach a dead end. The dissent would not "write." It was at this point that Mrs. Harlan contributed a dramatic touch to the history of the *Civil Rights Cases.*

When the Harlans had moved to Washington in 1877, the Justice had acquired from a collector the inkstand which Chief Justice Roger Taney had used in writing all his opinions. Harlan was fond of showing this to guests and remarking that "it was the very inkstand from which the infamous *Dred Scott* opinion was written." Early in the 1880's, however, a niece of Taney's, who was engaged in collecting her uncle's effects, visited the Harlans. When she saw the inkstand she asked Harlan for it, and the Justice agreed. The next morning Mrs. Harlan, noting her husband's reluctance to part with his most prized possession, quietly arranged to have the inkstand "lost." She hid it away, and Harlan was forced to make an embarrassed excuse to Taney's niece.

Now, on a Sunday morning, probably early in November of 1883, after Harlan had spent a sleepless night working on his dissent, Mallie Harlan remembered the inkstand. While the Justice was at church, she retrieved it from its hiding place, filled it with a fresh supply of ink and pen points, and placed it on the blotter of his desk. When her husband returned from church, she told him, with an air of mystery,

CIVIL RIGHTS AT WALLACK'S THEATRE.

SWELL DARKEY—*"Boss, I want a box."* MANAGER—*"Boxes all taken."* S. D.—*"Dress circle, then."* M.—*"All sold."* S. D.—*"Balcony?"* M.—*"House full. Nothing left but a corner in the gallery."*

Despite the 1875 law, many theatre owners continued to deny seats to Negroes, and Leslie's Weekly *applauded their actions.*

that he would find something special in his study. Harlan was overjoyed to recover his symbolic antique. Mrs. Harlan's gesture was successful, for as she relates:

The memory of the historic part that Taney's inkstand had played in the Dred Scott decision, in temporarily tightening the shackles of slavery upon the negro race in those antebellum days, seemed, that morning, to act like magic in clarifying my husband's thoughts in regard to the law . . . intended by Sumner to protect the recently emancipated slaves in the enjoyment of equal 'civil rights.' His pen fairly flew on that day and, with the running start he then got, he soon finished his dissent.

How directly the recollection of Dred Scott pervaded Harlan's dissent is apparent to anyone who reads the opinion. He began by noting that the pre-Civil War Supreme Court had upheld congressional laws forbidding individuals to interfere with recovery of fugitive slaves. To strike down the Act of 1875 meant that "the rights of freedom and American citizenship cannot receive from the Nation that efficient protection which heretofore was unhesitatingly accorded to slavery and the rights of masters."

Harlan argued that the Civil Rights Act of 1875 was constitutional on any one of several grounds. The Thirteenth Amendment had already been held to guarantee "universal civil freedom"; Harlan stated that barring Negroes from facilities licensed by the state and under legal obligation to serve all persons without discrimination restored a major disability of slavery days and violated that civil freedom. As for the Fourteenth Amendment, its central purpose had been to extend national citizenship to the Negro, reversing the precedent upheld in the Dred Scott decision; its final section gave Congress power to pass appropriate legislation to enforce that affirmative grant as well as to enforce the section barring any state action which might deny liberty or equality. Now, the Supreme Court was deciding what legislation was appropriate and necessary for those purposes, although that decision properly belonged to Congress.

Even under the "State action" clause of the Fourteenth Amendment, Harlan continued, the 1875 act was constitutional; it was well established that "railroad corporations, keepers of inns and managers of places of public accommodation are agents or instrumentalities of the State." Finally, Harlan attacked the unwillingness of the Court's majority to uphold the public-carrier section of the act under Congress' power to regulate interstate trips. That was exactly what was involved in Mrs. Robinson's case against the Memphis and Charleston Railroad, he reminded his colleagues; it had not been true before that Congress had had to cite the section of the Constitution on which it relied.

In his peroration, Harlan replied to Bradley's comment that Negroes had been made "a special favorite of the law." The war amendments had been passed not to "favor" the Negro, he declared, but to include him as "part of the people for whose welfare and happiness government is ordained."

Today, it is the colored race which is denied, by corporations and individuals wielding public authority, rights fundamental in their freedom and citizenship. At some future time, it may be that some other race will fall under the ban of race discrimination. If the constitutional amendments be enforced, according to the intent with which, as I conceive, they were adopted, there cannot be in this republic, any class of human beings in practical subjection to another class. . . .

The *Civil Rights Cases* ruling did two things. First, it destroyed the delicate balance of federal guarantee, Negro protest, and private enlightenment which was producing a steadily widening area of peacefully integrated public facilities in the North and South during the 1870's and early 1880's. Second, it had an immediate and profound effect on national and state politics as they related to the Negro. By denying Congress power to protect the Negro's rights to equal treatment, the Supreme Court wiped the issue of civil rights from the Republican party's agenda of national responsibility. At the same time, those southern political leaders who saw anti-Negro politics as the most promising avenue to power could now rally the "poor whites" to the banner of segregation.

If the Supreme Court had stopped with the *Civil Rights Cases* of 1883, the situation of Negroes would have been bad but not impossible. Even in the South, there was no immediate imposition of segregation in public facilities. During the late 1880's, Negroes could be found sharing places with whites in many southern restaurants, streetcars, and theatres. But increasingly, Democratic and Populist politicians found the Negro an irresistible target. As Solicitor General Phillips had warned the Supreme Court, what had been tolerated as the "fact" of discrimination was now being translated into "doctrine": between 1887 and 1891, eight southern states passed laws requiring railroads to separate all white and Negro passengers. The Supreme Court upheld these laws in the 1896 case of *Plessy v. Ferguson*. Then in the Berea College case of 1906, it upheld laws forbidding private schools to educate Negro and white children together. Both decisions aroused Harlan's bitter dissent. In the next fifteen or twenty years, the chalk line of Jim Crow was drawn across virtually every area of public contact in the South.

Today, as this line is slowly and painfully being erased, we may do well to reflect on what might have been in the South if the Civil Rights Act of 1875 had been upheld, in whole or in part. Perhaps everything would have been the same. Perhaps forces at work between 1883 and 1940 were too powerful for a Supreme Court to hold in check. Perhaps "Sumner's law" was greatly premature. Yet it is difficult to believe that total, state-enforced segregation was inevitable in the South after the 1880's. If in these decades the Supreme Court had taken the same *laissez-faire* attitude toward race relations as it took toward economic affairs, voluntary integration would have survived as a counter-tradition to Jim Crow and might have made the transition of the 1950's less painful than it was. At the very least, one cannot help thinking that Harlan was a better sociologist than his colleagues and a better southerner than the "irreconcilables." American constitutional history has a richer ring to it because of the protest that John Marshall Harlan finally put down on paper from Roger Taney's inkwell in 1883.

Alan F. Westin is an associate professor of public law and government at Columbia University. He is at present working on a biography of Justice John Marshall Harlan—who, incidentally, was the grandfather of a present Supreme Court Justice who bears the same name.

For further reading: The Constitutional Doctrines of Justice Harlan, by Floyd Barzillia Clark (Johns Hopkins, 1915); The Supreme Court in United States History, Vol. II: 1836–1918, by Charles Warren (Little, Brown, 1960); The Strange Career of Jim Crow, by C. Vann Woodward (Oxford University Press, 1958).

The beginning of the trial found a cocksure Hermann Goering (left) and his onetime crony, the demented Rudolph Hess, in good humor.

NUREMBERG:

The Fall of the  *Supermen*

Even as the horrors unfolded, it seemed difficult to connect them with the shabby figures in the prisoners' dock. And yet, these contemptible shadows had once been among the most powerful and corrupt men on earth. In a rare view from the bench, the U.S. judge at the war crimes trial of the twenty-one top Nazis records the last chapter of their evil careers. It is adapted from Mr. Biddle's forthcoming autobiography, *In Brief Authority*, to be published by Doubleday this fall.

By FRANCIS BIDDLE

After ten months of testimony which forever demolished the Nazi myth, the smiles had vanished, and two broken men listened grimly to the verdict.

65

THE JUDGES: *U.S.S.R., A. F. Volchkov (alternate) and I. T. Nikitchenko; Great Britain, Sir Norman Birkett (alternate) and Geoffrey*

On the twentieth of November, 1945, the trial began "in a high solemn moment of extreme importance," as the Soviet member, General I. T. Nikitchenko, put it. Geoffrey Lawrence, the British member, made a brief statement before the indictment was read as required by the Charter of the International Military Tribunal (it took nearly two days to read it in four languages). "It is the duty of all concerned," he said, "to see that the Trial in no way departs from those principles and traditions which alone give justice its authority and the place it ought to occupy in the affairs of all civilized states." Everyone was impressed with his dignity and sincerity; and the sense of authority—so thoroughly British in quality—that he brought to the courtroom largely accounted for the orderly days in court that followed. "Incidents" had been feared, but there were none. Germans were used to bowing their heads to authority.

The chief American prosecutor, Justice Robert Jackson of the Supreme Court, made an eloquent and moving opening statement. The wrongs here condemned, he began, were so devastating that "civilization cannot tolerate their being ignored, because it cannot survive their being repeated. That four great nations, flushed with victory and stung with injury, stay the hand of vengeance and voluntarily submit their captive enemies to the judgment of the law is one of the most significant tributes that Power has ever paid to Reason." We must never forget, he continued, "that the record on which we judge these defendants today is the record on which history will judge us tomorrow. If these men are the first war leaders of a defeat-

ed nation to be prosecuted, they are also the first to be given a chance to plead for their lives in the name of the law." The duty of the Tribunal, he said, was to apply the sanctions of the law to those who were guilty of the crimes charged. Civilization "does not expect that you can make war impossible. It does expect that your juridical action will put the forces of international law, its precepts, its prohibitions and, most of all, its sanctions, on the side of peace, so that men and women of good will in all countries may have 'leave to live by no man's leave, underneath the law.' "

Sir Hartley Shawcross, when he opened the British case on December 4, emphasized individual responsibility: "The State is not an abstract entity. Its rights and duties are the rights and duties of men. Its actions are the actions of men. . . . Politicians who embark upon a war of aggression should not be able to seek immunity behind the intangible personality of the State."

To me, François de Menthon's summary of the French case was more interesting than any, and in many ways more moving: more interesting because he sought to distinguish and to understand the German soul within the dark atmosphere of German action; more moving because he thought and spoke of Germans as members of a group to which all human beings belonged. The philosophy of the National Socialist party, he argued, had logically resulted in a war of conquest fought without respect for any human values. The vast organized criminality sprang from "a crime against the spirit," which aimed to plunge humanity back into barbarism—it was not the spontaneous savagery of a primitive race, but a reaction

Lawrence; United States, Francis Biddle and John J. Parker (alternate); France, Henri Donnedieu de Vabres and Robert Falco (alternate).

conscious of itself, utilizing for its ends the material means put at the disposal of mankind by contemporary science.

This doctrine, de Menthon pointed out, was based on the monstrous theory of racism. Its end was the absorption of the personality of the citizen into that of the State, and the intrinsic value of the human being was finally denied. Anyone whose opinions differed from the official doctrine was asocial and unhealthy. Humanism was condemned as decadent. Reason was replaced by the romance and the virility of war; violence became the test of manhood. National Socialism in modern Germany, he concluded, was the "ultimate result of a long evolution of doctrines," raising "inhumanity to the level of a principle."

General R. A. Rudenko, presenting the Russian case three weeks later, talked of crimes in the Slavic countries. He referred to the defendants, doubtless for some semantic reason of his own, as "Hitlerites" and "Fascists"—never as "Nazis"—with "the morals of cannibals and the greed of burglars." The prosecutors, he ended, were presenting the defendants with "a just and complete account which must be settled."

Of the defendants Hermann Wilhelm Goering was by far the most kaleidoscopic. He would occasionally forget himself in a blaze of anger. For so gross and heavy a human being he could move with extraordinary quickness. He sat in the corner of the defendants' box, a rug across his knees, the double-breasted light gray uniform of a Reichsmarshal that he had designed for himself now faded and baggy, and without decorations.

All the witnesses had to pass near him as they left the courtroom. When one German general who had given particularly incriminating evidence left the stand, Goering, leaning across Hess, remarked to Ribbentrop in a clearly audible voice: "That's one we missed after July 20" (July 20, 1944, when an attempt to assassinate Hitler failed and many anti-Nazi officers and aristocrats paid with their lives). And when another prosecution witness, Bach-Zelewski, a high ranking SS general formerly in command of antipartisan warfare on the eastern front, had finished testimony about the terrible atrocities committed there, Goering was suddenly on his feet. He spat in the face of the witness and shouted "*Schweinehund!*"—then seated himself, straightened his tunic, and beamed jovially at the military police who had rushed up. There was nothing to do.

On occasion Goering could be coolly and politely insolent, deferentially impudent. It was no wonder that this attitude—sly and quick and skillful—should irritate the cross-examining prosecutors. Once Jackson was cross-examining him about the minutes of the working committee of the Reich Defense Council in 1935, which contained a phrase translated as "preparation for the liberation of the Rhine." Goering suggested that Mr. Jackson had made "a great mistake." The phrase had nothing to do with any contemplated occupation of the Rhineland; it meant simply that the river should be kept clear in case of mobilization for defense against attack from the west, or from the east for that matter.

Jackson: You mean the preparations were not military preparations?

Goering: Those were general preparations for mobilization, such as every country makes.

Jackson: But were of a character which had to be kept entirely secret from foreign powers?

Goering: I do not think I can recall reading beforehand the publication of the mobilization preparations of the United States.

The answer was really innocuous, and Jackson should have let it pass. But he lost his temper. For some time Goering had been trying to put him off balance, and had

that famous trial, while Wilde laughed at him and the spectators egged him to further witticisms; held on until Wilde made his first break, and Carson had him against the wall, stammering and broken.)

"I respectfully submit to the Tribunal that the witness is not being responsive," Jackson appealed to the bench. It was "futile to spend our time if we cannot have responsive questions . . . this witness has adopted an arrogant and contemptuous attitude toward the Tribunal which is giving him the trial which he never gave a living

UPI

THE JUDGED: *On October 1, 1946, the indicted Nazis in the prisoners' dock tensely await the reading of their sentences. From the left, front row: Goering, Hess, von Ribbentrop, Keitel, Kaltenbrunner, Rosenberg, Frank, Frick, Streicher, Funk, and Schacht. Back row: Doenitz, Raeder, von Schirach, Sauckel, Jodl, von Papen, Seyss-Inquart, Speer, von Neurath, and Fritzsche. Their lawyers sit in front.*

finally succeeded. It was a long cross-examination, lasting a couple of days, and Jackson, already overburdened and tired, was feeling the strain. He made the initial mistake of not holding his witness psychologically and never letting him go. He should never have dropped his eyes from Goering's face. Instead, he kept occasionally looking at his notes while the witness was answering, as if he were not thoroughly prepared, and the impact was lost. (On the other hand, one of the British prosecutors, Sir David Maxwell-Fyfe, held on like a bulldog; held on without ever noticing the witness's impertinence, his sallies, his wit and sneers, which gradually died down; held on the way Edward Carson held on to Oscar Wilde during

soul," He asked that the witness be instructed to answer the questions yes or no, and leave explanations to the end of his testimony. I suggested to Lawrence that just then was a good time to recess, not to give an immediate ruling, and to let things cool off overnight. We adjourned—it was almost the usual time—and met in chambers. We were all of the opinion that witnesses after answering should be allowed to explain their answers at once—the usual practice—and not have to wait until the examination was over.

After the recess Jackson, profoundly upset, came to see me and my alternate, John J. Parker. He said we were always ruling against him, and intimated that I went out of my way to oppose him. He thought he had better resign from the trial and go home. We did our best to soothe and mollify him, to stroke his ruffled feathers by telling him how much we all admired him and how well he was conducting the trial.

At the time I thought it was merely his irritated reaction to Goering's calculated and telling impudence. Later I became convinced that some more enduring sense of failure or of disappointment haunted him. Missing some subtler value, he may have tried in vain to persuade his ambitious heart that the externals were all that counted. It is not improbable that appointment as Chief Justice of the United States would have eased that brooding misery. But I do not think any achievement would have altogether banished it.

In the eight years that followed Nuremberg, Jackson came nearer than he ever had to finding a serenity of mind that filled most of his conscious being—he loved his work on the Court, and his work was of a very high order—thoughtful, lawyerlike, and wise. He was deeply admired by the bar. His pungent style, personal and fresh, would frame his opinions for later generations. And if that was not enough it was a good deal. Only when his face was in repose did the inner light disappear, and the commonplace settle in, as if the emptiness had been waiting at the edges of his vitality.

Dr. Horace Greeley Hjalmar Schacht, Hitler's onetime minister of economics, was a witness of a different kidney. Wrapped in a Teutonic self-esteem which fitted him like a pair of suede gloves, he remained cool, never surprised, disdainfully self-reliant. He listened to each question, very straight and stiff in his five-inch collar, looking over and beyond the others, occasionally breaking into English. He sounded more like a professor reproving an overeager pupil than a prisoner fighting for his life. Had Mr. Justice Jackson taken a course in economics in school? Perhaps if he, Schacht, explained in simple language. . . .

He hated Goering with a scornful, jealous bitterness, for it was Goering who had forced him out of power. Goering, Schacht said, in an interrogatory,

endowed by nature with a certain geniality . . . was the most egocentric being imaginable. The assumption of political power was for him only a means to personal enrichment and good living. The success of others filled him with envy. His greed knew no bounds. His predilection for jewels, gold, and finery was unimaginable. He knew no comradeships. . . . In his personal appearance . . . one could only compare him to Nero, [appearing at tea once] in a sort of Roman toga and sandals studded with jewels, his fingers bedecked with innumerable jeweled rings . . . his face painted and his lips rouged.

And, Schacht added, his competence in the economic field was nil.

Frau Schacht, writing to her husband like any wife to any husband, told him that she was very well, only the toilet was out of order. She continued: "The prosecution speeches are terribly boring. All the Congo bestiality is being rehashed. Instead of the Gestapo and the SS being convicted here, the government, general staff, and even our brave G.I.'s [sic, in the translation] are being thrown into the same pot. Only Hitler and his cronies are deserving of death. A German court would have been better. . . . Take care of yourself, darling."

Cross-examination of course varied from nation to nation, and it was natural that the French should be less good at it than the British and Americans, for it is not a French technique. The Russian idea of cross-examination was to read a long incriminating question and then expect the defendant to admit everything. Thus the Soviet prosecutor, General Rudenko, cross-examined Alfred Rosenberg, the chief philosopher of the Nazi party and the Reichsminister for Hitler's vast empire in eastern Europe.

Rudenko: Do you admit that Nazi Germany, having prepared and pursued war against the Soviet Union, aimed at plundering the economic riches of the Soviet Union, the extermination and enslavement of her people, and the disarmament of the country? Answer briefly.

Rosenberg: No.

Rudenko (with sarcasm): You deny it? All right. Let us turn to a new document.

The Russians were used to co-operation from a defendant in their own country, and were rather put out by what, among themselves, they probably referred to as the careless preparation of the Americans. It was not to be expected that they would understand our judicial practice when the purposes of their trials were so different. The Russian trial must conform to the policy of the state, not oppose it. When, for instance, Rosenberg's lawyer applied for leave to call a witness to prove that the Soviets had employed slave labor practices in Latvia, Volchkov, the Russian alternate, was genuinely shocked that we should even listen to such a suggestion. To him it was libelous, and he said so: obviously libelous because it was an attack on his nation's sovereignty.

The Katyn Woods incident was typical of the Russian attitude. The inclusion in the indictment of the allegation that the Germans had massacred eleven thousand Polish officers in the Katyn Forest, on the banks of the Dnieper near Smolensk, was dictated solely by political considerations. Since there was no evidence that any defendant was remotely connected with the killings, the charge was irrelevant. Although he

HUNTER: *Supreme Court Justice Robert Jackson, chief U.S. prosecutor, spoke eloquently in summations, was less effective in cross-examination.*

had not seen the reports indicating that the Russians themselves might be guilty, Jackson sensed trouble, and did his best to persuade them to omit the charge. But Rudenko insisted on including it, leveling the charge against Goering as the highest-ranking officer among the defendants. In addition to reciting in detail the report made in 1944 by a Soviet commission, he produced three witnesses to establish German guilt. This took a week. When Rudenko had concluded, Goering's counsel petitioned the Tribunal to allow testimony showing that the Russians had killed the Polish prisoners. Rudenko indignantly opposed the motion.

When we came to consider it in chambers, General Nikitchenko threw all his weight behind the Soviet prosecutor. It was obvious that he attached great importance to our decision. I do not think that many things were expected of him by his superiors in Moscow, but there can be little doubt that they were eager to have the Tribunal brand the Germans as the perpetrators of those systematic and sordid killings.

We had permitted the Russians to introduce the hearsay evidence of their own self-serving report, and to support it with eyewitness testimony. The rest of us could not see why we should not allow the Germans direct evidence in their defense. The Soviet general's argument —and he spoke with conviction for a solid hour—was based on a phrase in the Charter which provided that the Tribunal need not require proof of facts of common knowledge, and that it might take judicial notice of official government documents for the investigation of war crimes.

Under this wording the Russian report was obviously admissible. But the phrasing of the Charter was in this case unfortunate; it coupled "facts of common knowledge" with "government documents," and in the Russian translation the two phrases might have interlocked.

Since government documents had been given special treatment, the Russian member argued, and recognized for what they were—statements of the true facts—how could their contents and conclusions be denied? We had no right to disregard the Tribunal's Charter, to flaunt its provisions.

For a time it seemed possible that Nikitchenko would withdraw from the Tribunal. And yet I thought he would not; he was too far committed, and such an action would appear an admission of guilt. But whether he bolted or not, we *must* let the defense call its witnesses, who, on behalf of the International Medical Commission formed by the Germans, had examined the corpses on April 29 and 30, 1943, two weeks after the discovery of the bodies of four thousand Polish officers, in uniform, in some cases shackled, with pistol bullets in the back of the neck. (The rest of the victims were never accounted for.)

We announced our decision the next morning. The Russian prosecutor immediately filed a petition for a rehearing of the question. During the entire trial, it was the only petition for reargument we received. Its language was somewhat intemperate: the court, Rudenko claimed, had misconstrued the Charter, violating its duty, and was grossly in error. The petition followed Nikitchenko's argument and indicated his co-operation.

The occasion warranted action. At our conference the next afternoon I asked my confreres to permit me to speak on a matter of the most vital importance to all of us, in that it concerned the integrity of the members of the Tribunal, their honor, and their competence.

The brethren were by now giving me their attention.

One of the prosecutors—I looked at General Nikitchenko—had filed a slanderous, arrogant, and unwarranted attack on the Tribunal, a body that would go down in history as the most important court in the world. I did not know what the practice would be in other countries. In mine the author of such an outrage would be cited for contempt. Perhaps in this very extreme case we should send him to prison immediately—there could be no defense.

"What do you think, General? Have you read General Rudenko's petition? What do you propose should be done?"

General Nikitchenko was taken off base. He mumbled that he had read the petition, but rather hurriedly. He had nothing to propose. The French were amused—they guessed what I was up to. The British were surprised—they had not been consulted.

I produced an opinion, drafted with a good deal of care the night before. With permission of the members I would read it. It could be read in open court immediately before General Rudenko was arrested.

I read the opinion. It denied the contention that government reports should be accepted as "irrefutable evidence of the facts found"—a contention "unsupported by the Charter and intrinsically unreasonable in itself." The Soviet prosecutor was in gross error in his construction of the Charter.

After a good deal of discussion, it was agreed—with the Soviet member's dissent, which called the opinion "flagrantly" in violation of the Charter—that the opinion should be filed but not made public. The presiding judge would simply announce in court that the petition had been dismissed. Nikitchenko no longer argued that German witnesses should not be called. His whole energy was directed to keeping the opinion of his three fellow judges from the press. He took seriously my suggestion that Rudenko be held in contempt; and as part of the "compromise" it was understood that no such action should be taken. He was pleased with the result. Two hours after we had adjourned, I got a pleasant note from him indicating that we understood each other—would I visit his country after the trial? He evidently had grasped the purpose of my tactic after he had had time to think.

The doctors called by the Germans were vigorously (though without damage to their position) cross-examined by the Soviets. But from that day on we heard nothing more about Katyn Woods. The Soviet prosecutor failed to mention these atrocities when he summed up the case against Goering. The evidence before us was inconclusive, and, as I have said, was unrelated to any defendant. Any mention of Katyn Woods was omitted when the judgment was under consideration.

But the careful investigation conducted by a committee of the United States House of Representatives in 1952 left little doubt that the Soviet NKVD had been guilty of the killings, as a step in the "extermination of Poland's intellectual leadership . . . to eliminate all Polish leaders who subsequently would have opposed the Soviet's plan for communizing Poland." The officers, many of them former professional men, government officials, and intellectuals, were captured when Russia invaded Poland. Fifteen thousand in all, they had been separated from the other prisoners and placed in three special camps, where they remained from the fall of 1939 until the following spring. During this period they were exhaustively examined to determine whether they could be converted to Communism. A few hundred were. The rest were presumably killed. It was testified that Stalin's son, when asked about the disappearance of the Polish officers, said: "Why those were the intelligentsia, the most dangerous element to us, and they had to be eliminated."

Perhaps no incident better illustrated the Russian attitude toward the trial than one that occurred early in 1946. It seemed that important visitors were constantly arriving in Nuremberg, among them the Soviet delegate to the United Nations (and onetime prosecutor in Stalin's infamous purge trials), Andrei Vishinsky.

Jackson gave him a large dinner at the Grand Hotel. After the usual flow of speeches and liquor, Vishinsky rose to his feet, genial, faintly bibulous, expansive. Vodka, he said, was the enemy of man, and should therefore be consumed. He wanted to propose a toast. He raised his glass, and we got up; and now he spoke very fast, so that it was hard to follow the interpreter: "To the German prisoners, may they all be hanged!" The judges, not quite taking in what he said, touched their lips to the champagne. But it did not take long for them to realize what they had done.

Parker came to my room that night to talk about it. It was *awful*, he thought. He hadn't understood. He would not be able to sleep, thinking about it.

I tried to brush it off, saying that no one had noticed what we did, it was a triviality that would be forgotten

UPI

CORNERED PREY: *Exuding arrogance to the end, Goering, the most important Nazi on trial, managed to unnerve Jackson with his effrontery.*

tomorrow—the essential was our approach to the prisoners. So far, that had been fair.

"Supposing Drew Pearson gets hold of it? Can't you see the heading: American judges drink to the death sentence of the men whom they are trying. . . ."

"Anyway, we're both in the same boat, John," I ventured.

"But you don't seem to care," he ended, shaking his head, looking at me mournfully. . . .

The Germans relish hierarchical distinctions, as conveyed by the long handles to their names. They like to record their doings and catalogue their possessions. At the notorious Mauthausen camp in Austria, they carefully registered the killings—and even recorded the fictitious causes to which they were attributed. Rosenberg's title and the meticulous manner in which he recorded his activities were typical of these two Teutonic impulses. He was known officially as "Delegate to the Fuehrer for the Total Supervision of Intellectual and Ideological Training and Education of the Party." Under his careful direction the Einsatzstab Rosenberg, organized to collect, arrange, and distribute plundered art objects, drew up a catalogue of sixty-eight volumes, beautifully illustrated, handsomely bound. On April 16, 1943, writing to his Fuehrer on the occasion of the great man's birthday, he reported in a brief "preliminary" manner the art-seizure action. He enclosed three volumes of "the provisional picture catalogues," and hoped "that this short occupation with the beautiful things of art, which are so near to your heart, will send a ray of beauty and joy into your careladen and revered life."

RACIST: *Julius Streicher's paper*, Der Stürmer, *incited anti-Semitic atrocities with its "propaganda of death."*

Adolf Hitler's ghost haunted the courtroom; we could all see its outline, standing contemptuously at Goering's elbow; frowning at Schacht as he spoke of the Fuehrer's enormous reading, of his juggling with his knowledge, of his diabolical genius as a mass psychologist. Julius Streicher, the Jew-baiting journalist who had been thoroughly under his spell, described Hitler emerging from a three-hour speech in the Munich beer cellar in 1921 "drenched in perspiration, radiant."

Field Marshal Wilhelm Keitel was impressed with the great man's knowledge of operations, of strategy, of organization, of the details of armament, of the equipment of all the armies, of the classic authorities on the science of war—Clausewitz, Moltke, Schlieffen. But General Alfred Jodl, summarizing his views in a last speech, said that the Wehrmacht was confronted with the impossible task of conducting a war they did not want, under a commander they did not trust, to fight a war with troops and police forces not under their command—by no means an inaccurate description.

We watched the defendants day after day, these drab men once great, most of them now turning on the Fuehrer who had led them to their brief spasm of violent triumph. A few were still loyal. Some felt that it was not "correct" to attack a dead man who had been head of the state. Others transferred their guilt to the man who, they said, was alone responsible, from whom, they pleaded, orders came that had to be obeyed; theirs but to do or die, they argued; how could there be a conspiracy, a meeting of the minds, as the prosecutors claimed, when one man's mind commanded all the others? . . .

Before long there developed, among the twenty-one accused, two groups under different leaders. The majority, particularly at first, before the worst of the testimony came out, followed Goering, from whom still emanated something of the old charm, the compelling ruffian power. Goering sustained the vanishing legend of the Reich, the intoxicating dream of a superior race that in the early days had clouded their minds and swollen their hearts with the excitement of the primitive, the barbaric romance of lawless men.

The prison psychologist, Dr. G. M. Gilbert, described the two rival groups in his book, *Nuremberg Diary*. He was with the prisoners constantly, talking to them between sessions of the Tribunal and in the evening. Dignity and stoicism was Goering's line, or at least a part of it, for he was a many-sided actor: the man of culture, bully, hunter of big game, buffoon, hero, mountebank; brilliant, eloquent, funny; tough, realistic (particularly in the eyes of the weak men), his vision even in his last days playing with the great future of a New Germany.

He detested, he asserted, anything that was undignified, but wished they all had the courage to confine their defense to simple defiance. And the others would laugh when he said: "Aggressive war? Ach! Fiddlesticks! What about the grabbing of California and Texas by the Americans? That was plain aggressive warfare for territorial expansion. When it is a question of the interests of the nation, morality stops. . . ." And his audience would nod, and smile; and their sense of guilt seemed less hard to

FALLEN EAGLE: *Rudolph Hess appeared in the same boots that he had worn on his mad flight to England in 1941.*

bear with this comforting assumption that all nations were alike.

But there was a second group who despised Goering. Jodl pictured Goering in the last two or three years of the war as disappearing from time to time, hunting, collecting art treasures, living his soft life at various castles. Admiral Erich Raeder, in a statement made while a prisoner of the Russians, said that "the person Goering had a disastrous effect on the fate of the German Reich"; that his vanity was unimaginable, his ambition immeasurable. He was always showing off, running after popularity—untruthful, selfish, greedy, jealous. The old-line diplomats, Baron von Neurath and Franz von Papen, considered Goering a bully and an upstart, and referred to him as "the fat one."

Goering liked to play one defendant against another, intriguing with these forlorn shadows as he had intrigued when they were great with power. When Ribbentrop had finished testifying, Goering whispered to Raeder: "He's all washed up." But, when the Tribunal recessed, he congratulated Ribbentrop on his performance. He could threaten his companions as well as encourage them, and most of them were afraid of him. When Albert Speer testified that in April, 1945, Hitler had told him that he had known for some time that Goering had failed, known that he was corrupt, known that he was a drug addict; and yet, cynically caring nothing for what might happen to the German people, had said that he was willing to let Goering negotiate the capitulation, Goering was furious. In a manner calculated to have Speer overhear him, he told some of the defendants in the dock that even if Speer came out of the trial alive, the *Feme* would assassinate him for treason, meaning the *Femegerichte*, the secret and brutal kangaroo courts organized after the First World War to punish persons suspected of informing on those working for the secret rearmament of the Reich. Speer laughed a little nervously when he repeated this in his cell to Gilbert.

Testifying, Goering was at his very best, speaking twenty-one hours on the stand without notes, touching lightly but effectively on his own youth—his father had been an intimate friend of Cecil Rhodes in South Africa; he had been the top German ace in World War I after von Richthofen was killed. He described in detail the demoralized and poverty-stricken Germany that he and his comrades returned to when the First World War ended. Germans had never had experience of a democracy, they did not want one; and in any event, the Allies deserted the Weimar Republic after it had been foisted on the country. The German principle had always been authority from above downward, and responsibility from below upward. Was it not natural that, looking about for patterns to follow, they should select two outstanding models? He paused, and let his eye travel over the bench. "The Roman Catholic Church," he continued, "and the U.S.S.R."

If Hermann Goering was the prime exhibit of Nazi evil, Albert Speer was the most humane and decent of the defendants. His straightforwardness and honesty, his calm and reasonable bearing, his awareness of the moral issues involved, impressed the members of the Tribunal. Speer, who was forty-one when he was tried, must have been a highly impressionable young German, idealistic and prone to hero worship, when he joined the party in 1932. Soon he became Hitler's personal confidant, and lavished a passionate admiration on his chief, if one can judge by the depth and bitterness of his ultimate disillusion.

A man of striking ability, Speer took charge of all war production. He was one of the few men trusted by Hitler. It was not until the last days that Speer began to question the character of his leader. Doubts had of course begun to

MAN OF CONSCIENCE: *Of all the defendants, the only one who genuinely seemed to comprehend the immensity of German war guilt was Albert Speer, Hitler's brilliant young armaments chief.*

cross his mind; but, working continually at his immense production job, aloof from the chicaneries and plots that eddied around the seat of power, he seemed, like so many other idealists, to have been unwilling to face a reality which was bound to destroy the faith that had meant everything to him.

Unlike the other men in the dock, he cared about Hitler primarily because he believed that the Fuehrer had led the German people out of their despair and impotence, and placed their feet on the path to recovery of national greatness. Speer was serious, deeply thoughtful, without humor, patient, his shoulders bowed under the shame of his people and the moral degradation to which he had helped to lead them. It was no wonder that hatred burned between him and Goering.

In the prison and in the lunchtime recess and when the defendants exercised, the moral struggle continued. Goering wanted the Nazi myth to persist. Even if they were to be found guilty, they could go down to posterity as heroic *Übermenschen*—supermen. He cornered poor, cowardly little Walter Funk in the exercise yard and told him he must reconcile himself to his fate, that he must stand by Goering and die a martyr's death. He need not worry because some day—even if it took fifty years—the German people would rise again and recognize them as heroes, and even move their bones to marble caskets in a national shrine.

But little Funk was not the martyr type, and cared little about what might happen to his bones. He blubbered a good deal. "I assure you," he confided to Dr. Gilbert, "I don't have the stuff for heroism. I didn't then and I don't now. Maybe that is the trouble." "I always came up to the door," he testified wistfully, "but was never allowed to enter." He was an unimportant little man. As president of the Reichsbank, he had made an agreement with Himmler to receive for deposit and handle the gold and jewels and currency that the SS brought in. "I was never told about gold teeth placed in my vaults," he whined on the stand. "How was I to know they included teeth wrenched from corpses?" Great carloads of the personal belongings of murdered Jews were brought to the bank from Auschwitz and Mauthausen; and there they were neatly sorted and arranged. The jewels and watches were sent to the Municipal Pawn Shops; the gold which had been extracted by a special detachment of SS men from the teeth of the corpses before they were cremated and the gold spectacle frames, to the Prussian mint, where they were melted into bars and returned to the Reichsbank. The notes and coin stayed in the bank. A systematic banker, little Funk. . . .

Day after day, as the trial went on, the horrors piled up—tortures by the Gestapo in France; "experiments" on prisoners, who died in agony; the gas chambers; the carefully planned liquidation of the Jews—hour on hour the twenty-one men in the dock listened, and the shame spread. Documentary films of concentration camps, showing bulldozers piling up huge stacks of naked, unidentifiable bodies, clearly unmanned most of the accused. After one day's evidence, the radio propaganda chief, Hans Fritzsche, was physically ill in his cell. And after the onetime Governor General of occupied Poland, Hans Frank, took the stand to make his cheap, dramatic confession—"a thousand years will pass and still this guilt of Germany will not have been erased"—Schacht observed to Gilbert that Goering's united front of loyalty and defiance seemed to have collapsed.

Speer tried in his testimony to destroy the Nazi legend forever. He prophesied that after the trial the people of Germany would despise and condemn Hitler as the proven author of her misery. The world will learn, he said to us, not only to hate dictatorship, but to fear it. For the totalitarian system in the period of modern technical development can dispense with all subordinate leaders, and mechanize them into mindless, uncritical recipients of orders.

The nightmare of many a man that one day technical developments might domineer entire peoples had merely been realized in Hitler's totalitarian system . . . The more technical the world becomes, the more the counter-balancing influence of the advancement of individual freedom and the individual's awareness of himself is essential. . . . This war ended on the note of radio-controlled rockets, aircraft developing the speed of sound, new types of submarines, torpedoes which find their own target, of atom bombs, and with the prospect of a horrible kind of chemical warfare. . . . In five to ten years this technique of warfare . . . will be able to destroy one million people in the center of New York in a matter of seconds with a rocket operated, perhaps, by ten men. Invisible, without previous warning, faster than sound, by day and by night [science] can spread pestilence among human beings and animals and destroy crops by insect warfare. . . . It is not the battles of war alone which shape the history of humanity, but also, in a higher sense, the cultural achievements which one day will become the common property of all humanity. A nation which believes in its future will never perish.

Speer had finished. He looked at us, and beyond us. Then very quietly he said, as if to prevent himself from sobbing: "May God protect Germany and the culture of the West." There was a long silence in the courtroom.

What about the other defendants? They were an assorted lot, perhaps hardly typical of the German people; most of them were small men who had once strutted in great places, men whose weaknesses may have attracted

HITLER'S LEGACY: *A frightful pyramid of bones and ashes, the fruit of one day's labor at the Weimar death camp, testified to the efficiency of a Nazi crematorium.*

them to Hitler. There were ruffians like Ernst Kaltenbrunner—"a bony and vicious horse" Rebecca West called him—who had succeeded the assassinated Reinhard Heydrich as chief of the Security Police, and who knew, as he said, that the hatred of the world was directed against him now that Himmler was no longer alive. A descendant of farmers and scythemakers, Kaltenbrunner stood six feet four, with the deep purple welt of a dueling scar across his face from ear to chin that seemed to swell and glow as he lied under cross-examination, denying his own signature when he was confronted with it, lying so palpably that his associates in the dock turned away from him the next day when they filed in. Even the pariah Streicher kept his face averted.

At one end sat Schacht in his tall collar and impeccable glow of self-righteous conceit; at the other, Julius Streicher, round-shouldered and moth-eaten, chewing gum, mumbling to himself, mean and sullen, mouthing his neurotic obsession about the Jews. None of the other defendants would talk with the lewd, sadistic Streicher. "A dirty old man," Rebecca West said of him, "of the sort that gives trouble in parks." In his paper, *Der Stürmer*, which was devoted to anti-Semitism, he had advocated "castration for race polluters." For Streicher, his trial was a "triumph of world Jewry." He believed himself a man whom destiny had placed in a position to enlighten the world on the Jewish question. He was certain that three of the judges were Jews, and practically the whole of the prosecution. They got uncomfortable when he looked at

them, he claimed, for he could always recognize the blood.

There was Hess, who once had been the number three man, his eyes sunk deep into the sallow cavern of his face, his reading ranging from Edgar Wallace to Goethe to Jerome's *Three Men in a Boat*, a bony scarecrow, wearing the same black field boots that he had worn on his famous "mission for humanity" when he proposed to the startled Duke of Hamilton what seemed to him such a reasonable solution of the war—Great Britain should hand back the German colonies and evacuate Iran, or else the Nazis would set up concentration camps and starve the population to death if the British attempted to carry on war from the Empire's outposts after the German invasion of England. There was little doubt that Hess' mind was rapidly deteriorating, a condition manifested by his indifference, his appearance of glazed abstraction, and his jerky, goose-step manner of walking. Although he suffered from amnesia, his capacity to follow the trial and to defend himself was not at first affected.

The defendants Keitel and Jodl were both connected with the OKW, the High Command of the Armed Forces, an interservice organization directly responsible to Hitler as Supreme Commander. Keitel was the chief of the OKW, with Jodl immediately subordinate to him. The British historian John Wheeler-Bennett, comparing them, believed that Keitel was a man of third-rate ability, with "ambition but no talent, loyalty but no character, a certain native shrewdness and charm but neither intelligence nor personality." Keitel particularly illustrated what

END OF THE MASTER RACE: *Transcripts discarded by newspapermen cluttered the empty testimony room of the Nuremberg courthouse after the final day of the trial.*

"training without education" did to the German military mind. The loyalty of both generals to Hitler was automatic. But Alfred Jodl, who came from a family of intellectuals, was an individual of high intelligence and vigorous personality, who deliberately subordinated his will to the Fuehrer's caprices and became one of his most idolatrous admirers.

Keitel looked like a cross between a battered but respectable coachman and one of the milder Anglican bishops. Obsequious in his cell, he would bow and scrape to a lieutenant. In court he sat upright and apparently composed in his shabby green uniform, stripped of decorations, always looking "correct." Marshal Keitel kept repeating on the stand in his defense that he had absolutely no "command functions," as if he considered that this description of his duties would absolve him of having faithfully carried out Hitler's orders to murder and to torture. Jodl, in a green coat and light blue trousers with red stripes, gave one the impression of strength and self-control. Like so many of the defendants, his attitude toward Hitler fluctuated between adulation and contempt.

Of the two admirals, Karl Doenitz, who had succeeded Raeder as head of the Navy, was the modern, highly trained technician. Admiral Raeder, a little man of an older generation, was born in 1876, entered the Navy at eighteen, and received the commendation of the Kaiser in 1910 when he was navigation officer of the Imperial Yacht *Hohenzollern*. Before retiring in 1943 he had been active in building up the German Navy and in the submarine warfare; but what particularly moved the Tribunal to impose on him a sentence of life imprisonment was his successful pressure on Hitler to invade Norway, in spite of Hitler's desire to keep Scandinavia neutral—one of the clearest acts of aggressive war in the record. Raeder was skeptical about what would happen to him; he hoped he would be shot, for at his age he had no desire to serve a prison sentence. He had already attempted suicide when in the hands of the Russians.

As the end drew near and the time for the delivery of the judgment and the sentences approached, even Goering's factitious gaiety grew thin and forced, and finally deserted him. Schacht looked tired and old, but his *sang-froid* never left him, and his back was like a ramrod. The tragedy of Germany had settled deep in the soul of Speer. Little Funk cried more, and Streicher kept on howling at night. The fear of death turned Ribbentrop to parchment, drawn and sallow between the points of chin and cheeks.

The reading of the judgment, a part of it by each member, was finished on the morning of October 1, 1946. Three men had been acquitted—Schacht, Fritzsche, and the wily old diplomat von Papen—and were moved to cells on the third tier. The others were waiting to hear their sentences. Fritzsche, Gilbert records, was overwhelmed: "Free . . . and not even sent back to Russia" (the Russians had captured him).

After a recess, the defendants who had been convicted were called to be sentenced. Standing there before us, they behaved like men. I felt sick and miserable. We had seen them day in and day out for a year. What right had I? . . . I knew they deserved it. Goering, who was the first to be sentenced, saluted when Lawrence pronounced his fate: "Defendant Hermann Wilhelm Goering, on the counts of the Indictment on which you have been convicted, the International Military Tribunal sentences you to death by hanging." Goering was glad that he had not got a life sentence, he later told Dr. Gilbert—those who were sentenced to life never went down in history as martyrs. How soon he would cheat the law, his thumb to his nose, pulling the phial of cyanide of potassium from some secret crevice in the folds of his vast flesh. . . . The slave-labor chief, Fritz Sauckel, when he got to his cell, said to Gilbert: "Death! I have never been cruel myself. But I am a man—and I can take it"—and burst into tears. Speer thought his sentence of twenty years was fair enough; he was glad Fritzsche had been acquitted . . . Kaltenbrunner, sentenced to death, tried to kiss his mistress through the grille of the visitors' room.

Admiral Raeder, who had been sentenced to life imprisonment, petitioned the Allied Control Council to change his sentence to death by shooting—the resistance of his body was low, he said, and his imprisonment would not last very long. But the Control Council had the power only to decrease sentences. At Spandau he acted as librarian, fussy and meticulous, liking to repeat the German saying: "A disorderly ship reflects incapability." He was fond of gardening. He was recently released, and is still living at eighty as I write this.

Twelve defendants* were condemned to death by hanging. Julius Streicher, a moment before he died, heiled Hitler, and from the gallows screamed, *"Purim, 1946!"* The cruel Persian minister Haman, too, had planned to kill the Jews living in his country, twenty-five hundred years ago. But when the Emperor Xerxes heard of his intentions, Haman and his ten sons were put to death on the very gallows that had been erected for their victims.

* Martin Bormann in absentia was the twelfth.

First the engines
posed, then drew a
mile apart; they
headed for each other,
the crews jumped
clear, and the crowd
leaned forward...

WHEN THE TWAIN...

There are many ways of running election campaigns in the United States. You can kiss babies, stand on your head, play the guitar, treat the electorate to cigars and hard cider, promise anything you like—or you can simply stay home on the front porch. As an occasional novelty you can discuss the issues, but stunts are more spectacular. Consider, for example, the event recorded here, which took place at Elyria, a short ride in the electric cars from Denver, Colorado, in 1896. Seeking to raise money for the "Free Silver" presidential campaign of William Jennings Bryan, his supporters in the "Silver State" staged this fine engine collision between two old narrow-gauge steamers of the Union Pacific Denver & Gulf Railway. On hand was the famous western photographer, William H. Jackson, whose pictures (now in the Ted James Collection) show

the whole dramatic sequence. In derision of the Republican candidate and his manager, the locomotives were renamed "Bill McKinley" and "Mark Hanna." A mile of special track was laid in a fenced-in area, with seats erected at the expected meeting point—but alas for well-laid plans! At the start, the Mark Hanna skidded on the rails. As a result, the Bill McKinley thundered past the paying spectators and had nearly reached the entrance to the grounds before it hit the other engine and filled the air with the roar of steam and flying metal. It was the standees and the free crowd outside the gate that got the best show. FIFTY CENTS FOR A FIZZ . . . A SPECTACULAR DISAPPOINTMENT! *cried the headline in the* Rocky Mountain News *the next day. It was perhaps not a case of cause and effect, but the real McKinley licked Bryan in the election that fall.*

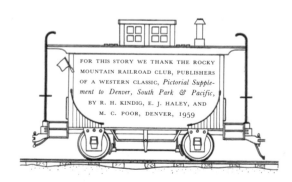

FOR THIS STORY WE THANK THE ROCKY MOUNTAIN RAILROAD CLUB, PUBLISHERS OF A WESTERN CLASSIC, *Pictorial Supplement to Denver, South Park & Pacific,* BY R. H. KINDIG, E. J. HALEY, AND M. C. POOR, DENVER, 1959

The battle between rebels and redcoats that should have

taken place at Bunker Hill was fought at Breed's instead.

It was the first of many costly mistakes for both sides

"*The decisive day is come*"

A selection from THE BATTLE FOR BUNKER HILL

By RICHARD M. KETCHUM

The port of Boston in June, 1775, resembled a medieval castle under siege. Since the engagements at Lexington and Concord on April 19, General Thomas Gage and some 5,000 British regulars had been bottled up in the town by a force of rebellious colonials that numbered between 8,000 and 12,000 men.

Though Gage had scant respect for his ill-trained and disorganized opponents, his situation was still dangerous, and it grew more so by the day. Two rolling swells of high ground—Dorchester Heights to the south and the Charlestown peninsula to the north—dominated the town, and were as yet unoccupied by either side; Gage knew that if the Americans ever marshaled the strength to take and hold them, his position would be all but untenable. Thus, early in the month, he decided to seize both points, an operation that was to begin on June 18.

But by a fortunate accident, American intelligence in Boston learned of Gage's plans, and the Committee of Safety—which, for the time being, served as the colonial high command—called for a quick countermove. On the night of June 16, about 1,000 men led by William Prescott of Massachusetts and Connecticut's impetuous hero of the French and Indian Wars, Israel Putnam, occupied the Charlestown peninsula, and with great stealth began to dig in.

Though they had been ordered to fortify Bunker Hill, a 110-foot-high knoll well out of range of the British land batteries on Copp's Hill in Boston, Prescott and Putnam chose instead to station their men on the lower and more exposed Breed's Hill. By dawn on the seventeenth, when H.M.S. *Lively* discovered their presence and began to shell them, the Provincials had built a redoubt six feet high.

Gage immediately held a council of war with the three officers who had recently been sent from England to help him quell the rebellion, Major Generals William Howe, Henry Clinton, and John Burgoyne. Clinton sensibly favored an attack on the narrow and unprotected neck of the Charlestown peninsula, just behind Bunker Hill, which would thus cut off the main American force. Gage overruled him. Whether out of pride in their crack regiments (which had been treated roughly in the retreat from Lexington and Concord) or contempt for the Provincial troops, the British high command decided instead to make a frontal assault on Breed's Hill.

The British plan was to land at the easternmost extremity of the peninsula, Morton's Point, and march on the redoubt. But the assault was delayed until midday, and the Americans were able to extend the exposed left side of their line to the Mystic River.

At one-thirty in the afternoon, Major General Howe, the senior officer under Gage, and the first contingent of redcoats began to embark in barges from Boston. What happened from that moment on is told in the stirring account that follows, taken from Richard M. Ketchum's book, *The Battle for Bunker Hill,* soon to be published by Doubleday.

The map at left details the fighting that surged around the American redoubt at Breed's Hill (Bunker Hill, for which the battle came to be named, was little more than a haven for rebel stragglers). British troops landed both at Morton's Point and near the burning village of Charlestown. After they were repulsed at the stone wall and the fence behind Breed's Hill, the redcoats assaulted the redoubt and finally drove the stubborn colonials from the peninsula.

81

The sun was blinding white, high in a clear sky. Inside the redoubt on Breed's Hill the dust hung like a motionless curtain, and men inhaled it with every breath they drew; sweat ran down their faces, little rivulets streaking the dirt and stubble of beard.

Across in the town of Boston and on all the surrounding hills, housetops were jammed with onlookers, spellbound by the great act of war unfolding before them, watching their familiar, quiet world erupt in a monstrous cacophony of noise and violence. Now all the warships were firing, their sides exploding in sheets of orange flame followed by clouds of greasy black smoke rolling across the water. As far away as Braintree, where Abigail Adams held the hand of a little boy who would be the sixth President of the United States, windows rattled from the distant concussions, and people who could not see what was happening listened and wondered, as she did, whether "The day—perhaps the decisive day—is come, on which the fate of America depends."

As the loaded barges shoved off from Boston's Long Wharf the British fire intensified, the gunners concentrating on the little rebel stronghold on Breed's Hill. Nine, twelve, and twenty-four-pound balls screamed across the water, throwing up spouts of dirt as they slammed into the hillside and the walls of the redoubt. One came so close to Captain Ebenezer Bancroft that it affected the sight in his left eye, leaving him with partial vision for the rest of his life, and moments later another sheared off an officer's head, splattering Colonel William Prescott with his brains. The Colonel stood there unconcernedly, calmly brushing away the blood and cleaning off his hands with a bit of fresh dirt.

But for one long, awe-struck moment the worn, dirty, shirt-sleeved farmers, staring over the walls of their earthen fort, had eyes and thought for only one thing. Before them was a sight the like of which no one had seen before, and whether they had an hour or fifty years of life remaining to them, it was something they would remember until they died. Even seasoned British officers, men who had seen the great armies of Europe line up before an attack, admitted they had never witnessed a scene such as this.

Across the third of a mile of water that lay between Charlestown and Boston came the barges—twenty-eight of them, two parallel lines of fourteen boats in single file, loaded to the gunwales with scarlet-coated British soldiers. The long white oars swept back and forth across the blue water in carefully ordered cadence, bringing the barges closer, ever closer, to the waiting rebels. In each of the two leading boats were six bright brass fieldpieces; behind them came the flower of the British army, nearly fifty men to a barge.

On and on the barges came, like lines of ancient galleys, sweeping ever nearer until men's faces were distinguishable beneath their hats; one by one the boats ground ashore, spewing troops onto the narrow beach at Morton's Point, big men, heavily loaded with muskets, blankets, and haversacks, who leaped out and jogged up the hill to form in long, disciplined lines. And as soon as they had unloaded their human cargo the barges turned again toward Boston and began their rhythmic crossing, this time to pick up some 450 additional foot soldiers, men in the red and blue coats of the Royal Regiment of Artillery, and the commanding officer of the assault force, Major General William Howe.

In all, 1,550 infantrymen landed in the first two waves—plenty of troops for the assignment as originally conceived—and thanks to the pounding guns of the fleet and the Copp's Hill battery, there was no opposition. But Howe perceived while he was en route across the Charles that the situation had changed drastically, and soon after arriving he sent a message back to Gage asking for reinforcements at once. Beyond the redoubt, along the top of Bunker Hill, Howe could see a huge, milling throng of colonials which he took to be reserves; and at just about the time he landed, he saw several bodies of men make their way through that crowd, hurry down the eastern slope of the hill, and take position on the flat shelf above the Mystic River. This put an end to his hopes for an unopposed flanking movement around the American left, and forced him to send for his reserves.

But in the meantime he unaccountably revealed his intentions by ordering George Clark, commanding the light infantry, to take an advanced position along the water's edge. "I was sent immediately forward with four companies of the corps of light infantry within about 400 yards of the works of the enemy, where we lay covered under the bank of the water and other banks extending to our left," Clark said. And here they lay on their arms until the attack began. Forming the other troops who had landed, Howe pushed three lines up to the top of Morton's Hill, and there the men unslung their haversacks and calmly ate dinner while the General waited for support to arrive. Once again, he was giving the rebels precious time to consolidate their defenses.

As soon as Prescott saw that the entire British force would land at Morton's Point, he ordered two field-pieces to "go and oppose them." Considering the number of guns available to him, and what they would face, it was a pitiful gesture, and Prescott knew it, but he had very few alternatives left now. He turned to young Captain Thomas Knowlton and told him to take his Connecticut men along in support of the artillery. Before long the detachment disappeared from sight beyond a clump of trees below Breed's Hill, and when they did not reappear where Prescott expected to see them, he could only assume that they had "marched a different course, and I believe those sent to their support followed, I suppose to Bunker Hill."

He was mistaken in this, but only partially. Captains Samuel Gridley and John Callender had their men seize drag-ropes and haul the four guns out of the redoubt in near panic, and indeed they made straightaway for Bunker Hill, claiming to all who questioned them that they were out of ammunition. But just as they were about to beat their teams into a gallop for the final dash to safety across Charlestown Neck, Putnam halted them, skeptical about their excuse, and throwing open the lids of their side boxes, found them full of cannon balls. He ordered them back to the redoubt, but as soon as he departed the officers and men ran, abandoning their guns.

Knowlton, however, did what Prescott ordered him to do, and although he may have misunderstood the Colonel's instructions as to the exact spot he was expected to defend, he occupied the first defensible position beyond the swamp that lay between Breed's Hill and the Mystic, forming a line which ran almost parallel to the extended breastwork and about two hundred yards behind it—a line bounded on one side by a road leading up Bunker Hill and on the other by the bank of the Mystic River.

As Lieutenant Dana, who was with Knowlton, described their position, they dug in "behind a fence half of stone and two rayles of wood. Here nature had formed something of a breast-work, or else there had been a ditch many years ago. They grounded arms, and went to a neighboring parallel fence, and brought rayles and made a slight fortification against musquet-ball." The result of their efforts was thus a double fence, with hay stuffed between the two lines of rails; and since the fence at the rear was on top of a low stone wall, with a ditch behind it, the position was stronger than it might seem. (One Englishman stated later that the completed breastwork was ten feet thick.)

There was still a gap between the rail fence and the breastwork, however, and although the swamp in front of it would hinder Howe's advance, someone—Knowlton, possibly, or reinforcements who came up later—had the presence of mind to construct here three little flèches, or V-shaped trenches, each one behind and slightly above the other.

By this time the one serious hole in the rebel lines—the open area between the end of the rail fence and the Mystic—was being filled in. The men Howe had seen running down the hill as he disembarked were the New Hampshire regiments of John Stark and James Reed. They had arrived at the crucial spot at precisely the right moment. Fortunately for the Provincials, the British barges had to make two round trips before Howe appeared on the scene, and this extra margin of time allowed John Stark to drive his men from Medford to the Charlestown peninsula and get them into line alongside the Mystic River at the right instant to foil Howe's plans.

Stark had had his troubles getting there, however. When he reached the Neck, it was crowded with men from two regiments who were afraid to cross in the face of fire from British ships in the river. The *Symmetry*, with eighteen nine-pounders, lay off Charlestown, and two floating batteries, or barges, each with one twelve-pounder, had hauled in near the milldam, and these three vessels were raking the whole Neck, preventing fainter hearts than Stark from crossing. This was a spot where courage and leadership counted, and John Stark possessed both. Without a moment's hesitation he started for Bunker Hill, ordering his men to follow; and when one of his officers suggested nervously that they quicken their pace, Stark fixed him with a withering eye and said, "Dearborn, one fresh man in action is worth ten fatigued ones," and walked on as before.

Israel Putnam was in command on Bunker Hill, but John Stark was not about to take orders from any Connecticut officer, nor did he need anyone to tell him what to do. He saw immediately the unprotected gap on the American left, pushed his men through the confused crowd on the hill, and led them at a trot down to the rail fence, where he joined Knowlton. Howe and the second contingent of redcoats were disembarking as they came down the slope, and Stark halted his men just long enough at the rail fence to deliver "a short but animated address," followed by three cheers, before having them extend the lines to the bank of the Mystic. Apparently some of the grass in these fields had been cut, for Henry Dearborn recalled how it lay in windrows and cocks, and the men gathered it up, stuffing it between fence rails as Knowlton had done in his sector, and repairing the fence as best they could. Their defense was scarcely ball-proof, but at least it gave the appearance of a breastwork and lent the men behind it some sense of security.

Adding to that feeling was the presence of Major Andrew McClary, a giant nearly six and a half feet tall, who was everywhere, bolstering their courage, giving encouragement and advice, seeing that all was in readiness. McClary was one of the most popular officers in the New Hampshire camp and was already something of a hero as a result of planning and leading a raid on the Castle at Portsmouth in December of 1774, four months before Lexington, when many of the muskets now carried by the New Hampshire regiments had been seized.

When Stark went over to the riverbank, where the fence ended, and saw that the steep bank fell off about eight or nine feet to a narrow beach, he realized at once that the British could march in complete safety along the water's edge, just below the little cliff. He hailed his "boys" and had them bring stones to make a wall right down to the river, and behind it he posted a triple row of defenders.

The American line was now as complete as it was ever going to be, and a British soldier scanning it from the vantage point of Morton's Hill would have seen four distinct elements from left to right: the redoubt, the breastwork, the rail fence, and the stone wall on the beach. (Between the end of the breastwork and the beginning of the fence was the gap in which the three flèches had been built.) The extreme American right consisted of two unfortified positions: a little cartway along a fence, between the redoubt and Charlestown, where a company of Little's regiment and a few other troops, among them Nutting's company, had been posted; and the main street of Charlestown, at the bottom of Breed's Hill, where three companies from Doolittle's, Reed's, and Woodbridge's regiments were stationed.

Behind the lines the situation was chaotic. Of nine Massachusetts regiments ordered out from Cambridge at the time of the alarm, only five were even partially represented on the field when the British attacked. Whole regiments and fragments of regiments went astray, wandering hither and yon because their commanders either misunderstood or disobeyed orders, or because the orders were uncertain or garbled to begin with. Some halted on the wrong side of the Neck, some went no farther than Bunker Hill, some headed in the wrong direction altogether. As one informant wrote Sam Adams after the battle: "To be plain it appears to me there never was more confusion and less command. No one appeared to have any but Col. Prescott whose bravery can never be enough acknowledged and applauded.—General Putnam was employ'd in collecting the men but there were not officers to lead them on."

It is difficult to imagine anyone who could have been spared less easily by the American high command than Joseph Warren, the thirty-four-year-old Boston doctor who was president of the Massachusetts Provincial Congress, an important member of the Committee of Safety, and a major general (though Warren had been so recently elevated to that rank that he had not yet officially received his commission). But Warren operated on the theory that major generals were supposed to fight, and minutes after the alarm sounded in Cambridge he was heading toward Charlestown with young Dr. Townsend, one of his medical students. Along the way someone must have recognized him and given him a horse, for two of his friends subsequently reported that Warren had overtaken them on horseback, exchanged greetings, and disappeared down the Charlestown Road. He reached the Neck between two and three o'clock, when the British cannonade was at its height, and made his way up the northwest side of Bunker Hill.

Putnam caught sight of Warren and came over to ask for orders, but the doctor refused, saying he had come as a volunteer. (Even in all the din and confusion, the contrast between these two must have occasioned a smile from the soldiers: Warren the man of intellect, tall and handsome in his best clothes; Old Put, the man of action, his shirtsleeves rolled up and a battered hat on his head.) After asking where he could be of most use, Warren went out to the redoubt, where Prescott also offered to relinquish his command. Again Warren refused, saying, "I have no command here; I have not received my commission," and, before taking his place in the line, he added a graceful word about how he would consider it a privilege to fight under Prescott.

While waiting for his reserve, William Howe saw the last sizable gap in the rebel line being filled up, saw what looked like a breastwork being erected on the American left, and concluded that some armed boats, sent up the Mystic to a point behind the rail fence, could drive the farmers out of their lines easily; so he ordered that useful pair of floating batteries over by the milldam to suspend action there and come around to the Mystic side. An hour or so earlier the plan would have worked, but the tides were with the Americans this day, and once the boats left their anchorage they could not get up either river again.

While this abortive maneuver was in progress, Howe turned his attention to his own left wing, fearful that the rebels in Charlestown might turn his flank or at least cause trouble during the attack. Snipers were beginning to annoy the British even at long range, so Howe posted a regiment on the left to protect his advance on that side and, turning to Admiral Thomas Graves, asked if the fleet could assist in routing the Provincials from the town. Graves asked eagerly if Howe wanted the place burned, and when the General agreed, signaled the ships to fire red-hot balls, which had been prepared for just such an eventuality, into the town. The battery, across the Charles River in Boston, was instructed to shoot carcasses—or balls containing combustibles—and before long a landing party came ashore at the eastern end of town and put the buildings to the torch.

And now Howe's reserve reached him; companies of grenadiers and light infantry landing between Morton's Point and Charlestown. (The boats carrying them were under the command of Midshipman Cuthbert Collingwood, who would one day succeed the dying Admiral Horatio Nelson at Trafalgar.) With them came the 1st Marines and the 47th Regiment, giving the English general some 2,200 rank and file, plus his artillery. As soon as they were in position Howe formed his men into two wings, with Brigadier General Robert Pigot commanding the left and himself the right.

The plan of attack was a simple one. Howe had sized up the American left as the weak point, for it was logical to assume that men who had taken a position only an hour or so earlier would have had far less opportunity to fortify than those who had been working all night in the redoubt. Therefore, the British right wing would strike the hammer blow, with the elite light-infantry companies advancing in columns along the narrow beach to overrun the low stone wall and sweep in behind the defenders at the rail fence, while the big grenadiers, supported by the 5th and 52nd regiments, advanced in two lines against the fence.

Although Howe had taken most of the picked men from the flank companies for what was to be the decisive attack, Pigot nevertheless had three companies each of light infantry and grenadiers, plus the 38th, the 43rd, and 47th regiments and the 1st Marines. Both wings were approximately equal, Howe having thirty-seven companies and Pigot thirty-eight, and Howe planned to roll up the American left and charge in on the redoubt from behind while Pigot moved around the fringe of Breed's Hill, skirting the houses of Charlestown, and struck the redoubt from that side. The British general saw no reason for the attackers to stop and fire: the assault would be made with the bayonet alone.

About three o'clock in the afternoon the long lines of British infantry stepped off, their advance heralded by a sharp cannonade from two twelve-pounders on Morton's Point; while out in front, one of the grenadier companies pushed forward the little sixes for closer work. Almost at once these light guns were in difficulty; there was trouble getting them through the soft clay and swampy ground at the foot of Morton's Hill, and the gunners discovered to their dismay that the side boxes were filled with twelve-pound instead of six-pound balls.

Howe sent immediately for the proper balls, ordering the substitution of grapeshot until they arrived; but the range was too much for grape, and the guns were temporarily worthless. However, the ships' cannon, those on Copp's Hill, and the twelve-pounders on Morton's Hill concentrated their fire on the rebel works, and with this support the redcoats pushed forward.

Off to the right along the narrow strip of beach, the light infantry led the way, with a company of the famous Welch Fusiliers, the 23rd Infantry, out in front. Four abreast, eleven companies marched in precise columns, their bright uniforms sparkling in the sun, bayonets gleaming, the men's eyes trained on the low stone wall in the distance.

To their left came the long, double battle line, stretching nearly halfway across the peninsula. This was a parade march, with ten companies side by side— some 300 scarlet-coated men—marching forward on the broad front, followed by another wave of ten companies in step behind them, and these two lines were duplicated farther to the left, as Pigot's wing began its advance. The day was fiercely hot, and the British soldiers, steaming in red woolen uniforms, were loaded with three days' provisions, blankets, cartouche boxes, ammunition, and muskets—about the same weight as if they carried a good-sized deer on their backs.

The unmown grass through which most of the battle line had to maneuver was thick and high, reaching almost to the waist in places, and concealing—as anyone who has walked through an uncut New England meadow knows—countless rocks and potholes. There were ten or twelve stone walls and fences to clamber over, a brick kiln, swamps, and sticky clay; and for Pigot's troops the going was all uphill. Portions of the lines stopped at times, slowed by fences (General John Burgoyne said they "met with a thousand impediments from strong fences," and Howe complained that these obstructions broke the perfection of his line); again they halted to let the fieldpieces come up.

At the southwestern end of the peninsula Charlestown was in flames, "a most awful, Grand and Melancholy Sight," one young loyalist said. To John Burgoyne, watching from Copp's Hill, it was

one of the greatest scenes of war that can be conceived: if we look to the height, Howe's corps, ascending the hill in the face of intrenchments, and in a very disadvantageous

85

ground, was much engaged; to the left the enemy pouring in fresh troops by thousands, over the land; and in the arm of the sea our ships and floating batteries cannonading them; straight before us a large and noble town in one great blaze—the church-steeples, being timber, were great pyramids of fire above the rest; behind us, the church-steeples and heights of our own camp covered with spectators of the rest of our army which was engaged; the hills round the country covered with spectators; the enemy all in anxious suspense; the roar of cannon, mortars and musketry; the crash of churches, ships upon the stocks, and whole streets falling together, to fill the ear; the storm of the redoubts, with the objects above described, to fill the eye; and the reflection that, perhaps, a defeat was a final loss to the British Empire in America, to fill the mind—made the whole picture, and a complication of horrour and importance, beyond any thing that ever came to my lot to be witness to.

Behind their earthworks and flimsy fences the rebels watched and waited; men faint with hunger and fatigue, dirty farmers in floppy felt hats and homespuns, fingering their muskets nervously, feeling instinctively for spare cartridges, anxiety and disbelief welling up in their dry throats as the finest infantry in the world moved closer and closer, threatening to engulf them.

Just behind the firing line, officers crouched low and moved swiftly back and forth, passing the word to shoot low, to wait for the order to fire, to pick out the officers and aim for the crossing of the belts, to wait until they could see the whites of their eyes. And the red tide moved slowly nearer, near enough now so the defenders could distinguish faces beneath the tall pointed helmets, make out rows of shining buttons and belt buckles. Now and again there was a strange moment of silence—the big guns had stopped firing, for fear of hitting their own men—broken only by the steady dull thump of marching feet, the swish of long grass as 2,000 men pushed through it, the crackle of flames and the occasional splintering crash of a building in Charlestown.

Over along the beach Howe's light infantry moved forward rapidly across the level, unobstructed sand, and the long, lancelike column was almost close enough to charge. Still there was silence behind the rebel barricade, no sign of movement. The British were only two hundred feet away, then one hundred, now fifty, when a row of dull musket barrels leveled along the stone wall, a nasal New England voice twanged, and the wall disappeared in a sheet of flame and oily black smoke. The blast of fire tore apart the leading ranks of Fusiliers, and as the rows behind closed up they were shattered by the violent hail of bullets. Officers fell, men spun around and dropped headlong into the shallow water, and the column stopped, recoiled, then came on again, the King's Own Regiment shoving through the broken Fusiliers, clambering over the

dead and wounded, only to be met with that withering fire from the wall.

Officers' voices shouted hoarsely through the din, ordering the men forward, but with each advance the men in the lead simply melted away, falling grotesquely and piling up the awful carnage on the narrow beach until there was nothing to do but turn back. And turning back, the men began to run, terror-stricken, pelting along the wet sand toward safety. Behind them the defenders peered through thick smoke that lay like a greasy blanket around the stone wall, saw their flight, saw the fallen "as thick as sheep in a fold," the dead floating crazily on the ebbing tide, the shallow water lapping red against the sand.

The flank attack on which Howe's hopes rested was shattered. The Reverend Peter Thacher, watching from across the Mystic, saw the light infantry retreat "in very great disorder down to the point where they landed, & there some of them even into their boats; at this time their officers were observed by spectators on the opposite shore to . . . use the most passionate gestures & even to push forward ye men with their swords."

There could be no retreating; even though the flank attack had failed, Howe could still rely on his long line of grenadiers and regulars and a direct frontal blow. These men, advancing steadily on the level above and out of sight of the beach, had been delayed by the long grass, the rough terrain, and the fences, and just as they were readying for the charge heard the great roll of musketry off to their right and the screams of wounded men. There was one last fence to cross before they could attack, and they had just climbed over it and were forming for the charge when a few defenders behind the rail fence opened on them.

Lieutenant Knowlton had given orders not to fire until the enemy came within fifteen rods, and then not until the word was given. But Lieutenant Dana told his friend John Chester that he had been the first to shoot,

and that he did it singly, and with a view to draw the enemy's fire, and he obtained his end fully, without any damage to our party. Our men then returned the fire, well-directed, and to very good effect, and so disconcerted the enemy that they partly brok[e and re]treated. Many of our men were for pursuing, [but by] the prudence of the officers they were prevented lea[ving so] advantageous a post.

It is hard to believe that Dana alone forced the red-coats to fire, but whatever the cause, apparently they halted to do so and were struck at that moment by a blast from the rail fence that shattered their lines. By some miracle, Howe was not hit, but all around him officers and aides were down, and his tough grenadiers fell by threes and fours, leaving gaping holes in that once-perfect line. They loaded again and fired, but their aim was hurried and the bullets went over the Americans' heads, while the standing, red-coated figures made perfect targets for the defenders, sighting their pieces along the fence rails. The line of regulars, coming up behind the grenadiers, was torn apart by the murderous volleys, and at last both lines turned and ran out of range, too badly mauled to continue.

Off on the British left, Pigot's lines had advanced slowly in what was intended only as a feint or delaying action while Howe's forces should punch through on the right. In spite of the raging fire in the streets of Charlestown, rebel skirmishers there harassed Pigot so effectively that his men were unable to mount a real attack on the redoubt, and when he saw what had happened to Howe he called them back.

Along the entire British line the attack had failed, and behind their bulwarks ragged defenders jumped with joy at the sight of those red-coated backs dashing for cover. In every section of the rebel defenses, the troops were jubilant with the realization that they had repulsed a frontal attack by the famous regulars. Ninety-six British dead lay on the beach alone, and all over the field were prone bodies, scattered pieces of equipment, the wounded crying piteously, some trying to drag themselves back to their lines. And it had all been done so easily, at so little cost to the Americans. Only Prescott and Stark and a few others knew that the battle was far from won, and they walked back and forth along their lines, praising the men, encouraging them, reminding them that there would be more work to do.

By now Prescott had only 150 men left in the redoubt; another 200 or so were behind the breastwork, and there were between 400 and 500 along the American left, posted behind the rail fence and the stone wall—a force, in all, of no more than 800 or 1,000. Peering out of the redoubt, Peter Brown estimated that there were only 700 "of us left not deserted"— a bitter reference to those who had slipped out of the lines since the night before. To the rear, on Bunker Hill, there were hundreds of men, probably as many or more than there were at the front, but few of them had any intention of moving into a more exposed position.

Within a quarter of an hour Howe had re-formed his broken ranks, but this time he decided not to assault that murderous stone wall on the beach. He regrouped what was left of his light infantry and put them into line with the grenadiers on the right; these flank companies would storm the rail fence, supported as before by the 52nd and the 5th regiments. This time, however, Pigot was expected to carry the redoubt on his own, without waiting for a flanking movement from the right.

Again the scarlet lines, thinner now, but with the foot soldiers still carrying full packs, stepped off, and as in the first attack there was no fire from the rebels until the foe was within a hundred feet. Then came that devastating explosion of musketry, then another and another, the Americans firing and loading as fast as they could. "As we approached," a British officer said, "an incessant stream of fire poured from the rebel lines; it seemed a continued sheet of fire for near thirty minutes." Howe's right was being raked from behind the rail fence by Samuel Trevett's cannon, which ripped into the advancing grenadiers. Meanwhile, the same British officer reported that,

Our Light-infantry were served up in Companies against the grass fence, without being able to penetrate—indeed, how could we penetrate? Most of our Grenadiers and Light-infantry, the moment of presenting themselves lost three-fourths, and many nine-tenths, of their men. Some had only eight or nine men a company left; some only three, four, and five. On the left, Pigot was staggered and actually retreated. Observe, our men were not driven back; they actually retreated by orders.

Once again Howe saw his men thrashing through the long grass and climbing over fences in the face of the American volleys, saw his grenadiers and light infantry try to fire, then crowd together in a confused mass, only to have the oncoming second line plow into them from behind. As he confessed later, "The Light Infantry at the same time being repulsed, there was *a Moment that I never felt before*." (Prescott remembered seeing Howe standing almost alone, surrounded entirely by dead or wounded.) It was inconceivable; the vaunted British infantry could not get close enough to drive home a charge with the cold steel, but were mowed down as if by a giant scythe as they struggled to advance. It was too much to endure, and suddenly the decimated ranks turned and ran again.

From the housetops and steeples of Boston, loyalist and patriot alike watched breathlessly while that ribbon of scarlet and white ascended the hill a second time. As they looked, there was an orange flash like "a continual sheet of lightning" along the string of earthworks, and even before the sound (one observer described it as "an uninterrupted peal of thunder") reached them from across the water, the ribbon of toy soldiers was struck, and shivered as in a high wind, then crumbled into ruin. Where there had been a solid row of figures, now there was only a jagged line; on the ground was a narrow carpet of red, many of whose parts were still and silent, with here and there a twisting, writhing movement. Now and then an arm waved back and forth, helpless and appealing; single figures half-rose from the heap of bodies and sank back again as the living pushed on toward the breastworks, were hit again, and then surged back toward the water's edge, trampling dead and wounded in their haste.

In his own straightforward way, Colonel William Prescott told what happened in the American redoubt:

The enemy advanced and fired very hotly on the fort, and meeting with a warm reception, there was a very smart firing on both sides. After a considerable time, finding our ammunition was almost spent, I commanded a cessation till the enemy advanced within thirty yards, when we gave them such a hot fire that they were obliged to retire nearly one hundred and fifty yards before they could rally.

In the frightful confusion of disaster, the British wounded were taken aboard the waiting boats and ferried across to Boston. The hillside was strewn with the dead and the dying, and from every section rose the pitiful moans and cries of the wounded. There are reports that some of Howe's officers begged him not to attack again; he was faced with the choice of abandoning the attempt altogether or of trying another frontal assault, for the tides would not permit him to land in the Americans' rear even if he wanted to do so. He had seen what a direct attack cost, but he decided to try at least one more; and to execute it he needed more men. So while his battered units re-formed along the banks of the Charles, Howe sent a message to Clinton requesting reinforcements. Gage had made Clinton responsible for supporting Howe with troops as he needed them, and Clinton had already sent the field commander reserves in time for his first attack; now he dispatched the 63rd Regiment and the 2nd Marines.

But further inactivity was more than Clinton could stand; he and Burgoyne had been at the Copp's Hill battery from the beginning, watching the flow of events on the opposite shore, and when he saw the complete collapse of Pigot's left and the wounded gathering leaderless on the shore, he acted. Telling Burgoyne to explain to Gage why he had left without orders, he commandeered a boat and was rowed toward Charlestown. As they landed north of the town, two men in his boat were wounded, proving that there were still some rebels in the stricken village, but Clinton ignored the opposition and "collected all the guards and such wounded men as could follow—which, to their honour, were many—and advanced in column with as much parade as possible to impress the enemy." With Henry Clinton in the lead, this heroic little company of invalids made its way back to the battlefield to rejoin Pigot and fight once more.

In the rebel works there had been another scene of elation when the redcoats retreated for the second time, and during the long interval occasioned by Howe's regrouping and wait for reinforcements, the Americans began to doubt if he would attack again. Then, with renewed signs of British activity, the defenders looked to their ammunition and suddenly realized they were virtually out of powder. Some men had used all theirs, others had but a few shots left, for in the hectic moments when the British lines loomed ever closer they had fired not in volleys, but as fast as they could reload and discharge their weapons—often three or four shots a minute—and now the powder supply was almost exhausted.

To the rear the scene was as chaotic as ever. Troops were milling around beyond the Neck, afraid to run the gantlet of cannon fire, while hundreds more were wandering about leaderless atop Bunker Hill. Old Put was doing his best to get units into action, and on the safe side of the hill he came across one outfit whose commander, Colonel Samuel Gerrish, "unwieldy from excesssive corpulence," lay prostrate on the ground, pleading exhaustion. According to one of Gerrish's men, the moment they came in sight of the enemy "a tremor seiz'd" the fat colonel and "he began to bellow, 'Retreat! retreat! or you'll all be cutt off!' which so confus'd & scar'd our men, that they retreated most precipitately." Putnam ordered Gerrish to collect his wits and his soldiers and lead them to the lines, even threatening some of them and slapping them with the flat of his sword, but he could do nothing.

John Chester, captain of the Wethersfield, Connecticut, company that had decided to cover its bright blue and red uniforms with drab clothes before marching out of Cambridge, arrived at the Neck in time to witness the confused scene:

When we arrived there was not a company with us in any kind of order, although, when we first set out, perhaps three regiments were by our side, and near us; but here they were scattered some behind rocks and hay-cocks, and thirty men, perhaps, behind an apple-tree, frequently twenty men round a wounded man, retreating, when not more than three or four could touch him to advantage. Others were retreating, seemingly without any excuse, and some said they had left the fort with leave of the officers, because they had been all night and day on fatigue, without sleep, victuals, or drink; and some said they had no officers to head them, which, indeed, seemed to be the case.

Chester saw one entire company deserting, led by its officers. He shouted to the company commander, asking why he retreated, but was ignored, upon which Chester halted his own men, ordered them to cock their muskets, and informed the other officer that he would open fire unless he took his men back to the lines. The deserters immediately about-faced and headed for action.

On Breed's Hill the grisly task of bringing off the dead and wounded had begun. In comparison to British losses, those of the Americans were slight, but a number of officers and men were down. Colonel Brewer, whose men had taken a position between the breastwork and the rail fence, was hurt, and so was Colonel John Nixon, who was carried off the field with a serious wound.

Major Willard Moore, who had taken command of Ephraim Doolittle's Massachusetts regiment in the absence of its colonel and lieutenant colonel, had been wounded in the thigh, and as his men were carrying him up Bunker Hill he was hit again. He pleaded with someone to bring him water but there was none to be had, and he lay there in agony, telling his men to look after themselves. A sergeant saw two boys standing nearby and told them to run and get some rum. "Major Moore is badly wounded," he said. "Go as quick as possible." One of the youngsters was Robert Steele of Dedham, a drummer in Doolittle's regiment who had beat his comrades into line that morning to "Yankee Doodle"; the lad with him was Benjamin Ballard. A glance at the flames of Charlestown told them there was no hope of finding anything in that quarter, so they hurried off toward the Neck.

The *Symmetry* was still firing, and as they raced across the little isthmus they heard the balls fly overhead. On the other side they located a store which appeared to be deserted, so Steele stamped on the floor and called out, asking if anyone was there. When a man's voice answered from the cellar, Steele said they wanted rum. No reply. After a moment Steele called again, asking the man why he stayed in the cellar. "To keep out of the way of the shot," came the honest answer, and then, "If you want anything in the store, take what you please."

So Steele took a two-quart earthen pitcher and filled it with rum, Ben Ballard drew a pail of water, and they set off for the front lines again, passing through throngs of skulkers on the safe side of the Neck and atop Bunker Hill, and arriving at the entrenchment just as the British prepared to advance for the third time. "Our rum and water went very quick," Robert Steele noted.

Dozens of British officers had been killed or maimed, and the hillside was covered with dead and wounded who were too close to the rebel defenses for anyone to rescue. Major Spendlove, who had served forty years in the 43rd Regiment, received a mortal wound during the second charge, and his command was taken over by John Gunning, who had applied that very morning for a vacant majority in another regiment. Among the light infantry, which had borne some of the heaviest fighting, Captain Edward Drewe of the 35th was hit in the shoulder, thigh, and foot; Lieutenant Massey was shot through the thigh; Bard, the third officer of the same outfit, was badly hurt; and the non-coms were virtually wiped out.

Captain Lyon of the 35th, whose pregnant wife had watched the course of the fighting from the Boston shore, was loaded into a boat and taken back to be nursed by the grief-stricken woman; but, like Drewe and Bard, he died of his wounds. By the end of the day, this light company of the 35th Regiment was without a single officer, sergeant, or corporal, and the command fell to the senior private, who led the five remaining men. All told, the grenadiers and light infantry lost nearly seventy per cent of their strength.

Howe, preparing for the third assault, was substantially without aides or staff, so many had fallen in the first two charges. One aide, Thomas Hyde Page, was hit in the ankle and later lost the leg; Lieutenant Jordan, a naval aide, was dead with a bullet through his head. Even Howe's batman, Evans, who had followed him doggedly all over the field with refreshments, had had a wine bottle shot out of his hands, and was nursing a badly bruised arm. However, the British commander now had 400 fresh troops of the 2nd Marines and the 63rd Regiment for support, and more significantly, he had decided to vary his tactics. At last he allowed the men to remove their packs and leave behind all superfluous equipment.

This time his troops were to march most of the way in column before deploying for the final bayonet charge, and he shifted the weight of his line to the left, sending what remained of the grenadiers and the 52nd against the breastwork instead of the rail fence, leaving only a few troops to make a demonstration against the latter works. To support the assault he brought up his artillery, stationing the guns where they could rake the American lines with grape, and as the cannon moved forward, the third British attack got under way, the long columns slanting up the hillside into a lowering afternoon sun.

Ahead of them the rank grass was snarled and trampled, the green strands streaked red with blood and patches of scarlet cloth, and the entire rim of the slope was pockmarked with depressions where fallen men lay, most of them still and silent, a few thrashing in agony, begging a comrade for help. Many of the marchers wore bandages or a rough sling, and as the drums beat they headed up the hill through the low-lying smoke, faces set, their hearts pounding, dreading the resumption of that withering blast from the rebel lines.

An Ipswich man remembered that "they looked too handsome to be fired at; but we had to do it," and another American told how the British "advanced in open order, the men often twelve feet apart in the front, but very close after one another in extraordinary deep or long files. As fast as the front man was shot down, the next stepped forward into his place; but our men dropt them so fast, they were a long time coming up. It was surprising how they would step over their dead bodies, as though they had been logs of wood." There was no need to wait for a chance to fire, one rebel said; all you had to do was load and there would be a mark at hand, as near as you pleased.

But running out of targets was scarcely the problem. Behind the rampart, men with powder-blackened faces bit the end off their last cartridge, rammed it home, pulled the trigger, and then looked around for something else to shoot. Some were firing nails or little scraps of metal picked up off the ground, others grabbed handfuls of rocks and began hurling them at the oncoming enemy, desperately trying to prevent that terrible gleaming forest of bayonets from coming any closer.

Captain George Harris, leading the grenadiers of the 5th Regiment up the slope, scaled a little rise between the breastwork and the redoubt, was pushed back, and on the third attempt was grazed on the top of his head by a ball. As he fell backward he was caught by his lieutenant, Lord Rawdon, who called four soldiers to help him to safety. Three of the men were hit as they took him back down the hillside, and Harris told them irritably, "For God's sake, let me die in peace."

Somehow they got him out of gunshot to safety, and Harris' servant, who had been searching frantically for him, came running up just in time to get his master into the last boat then available for the wounded. Although it was jammed, they took Harris aboard, faint and shivering from shock, and shortly after he arrived in Boston a surgeon performed a trepanning operation on him, which the stolid Englishman watched by means of mirrors.

Atop Breed's Hill the fighting raged on toward its fiery climax. Despite the barrage from the British fieldpieces, no breach had been made in the American defenses. Then suddenly, Lord Rawdon said,

our men grew impatient, and all crying 'Push on, push on,' advanced with infinite spirit to attack the work with their small arms. As soon as the rebels perceived this, they rose up and poured in so heavy a fire upon us that the oldest officers say they never saw a sharper action. They kept up this fire until we were within ten yards of them; nay, they even knocked down my captain [Harris], close beside me, after we had got into the ditch of the entrenchment . . . There are few instances of regular troops defending a redoubt till the enemy were in the very ditch of it, [yet] I can assure you that I myself saw several pop their heads up and fire even after some of our men were upon the berm [the top part of an earthwork—*Ed.*] . . . I received no hurt of any kind, but a ball passed through a close cap which I had.

Lying on the outside of the redoubt, under the protection of its wall, Rawdon called out to young Ensign Hunter of the 52nd to show him how narrowly he had missed death. Another officer, Major Williams, was badly wounded, and Rawdon asked Hunter to go and find a surgeon to tend him; but Hunter, who had just seen Harris' rescuers shot as they carried him off, "had sense enough to know that I was much safer close under the works than I could be at a few yards from it, as the enemy could not depress their arms sufficiently to do any execution to those that were close under, and to have gone to the rear to look for a surgeon would have been almost certain death."

Samuel Webb took his place in the American line just as the fighting reached its peak and, looking around at his dead and wounded countrymen, had "no other feelings but that of Revenge." It was a good thing he had the stomach for fighting; five or six more Americans dropped within five feet of where he stood, and a musket ball grazed his hat. Webb saw Gershom Smith of his company go down. Edward Brown, who was at Smith's side, fired his own gun, then reached for Smith's and shot it. At that moment bayonets loomed over the breastwork, and the regulars began pouring in. Brown leaped for an enemy, seized his musket, and killed him with it on the spot.

 At the far left end of Pigot's line, which had swung around the west side of the redoubt in order to flank it, the British marines ran into the same shattering fire that had characterized the entire American defense. As they fell into confusion, most of the marines began to fire at the works instead of charging, and Adjutant Waller had all he could do to keep two companies in formation. Major John Pitcairn, who had commanded the British at Lexington in April, was attempting to rally his men; they heard him shout that the enemy had abandoned the fort, heard a boy call from behind

the wall, "We are not all gone!" And at that moment, men said later, a Negro named Salem Prince shot Pitcairn through the head. He fell into the arms of his son; close by him a captain and a subaltern were down, and Waller realized that

had we stopped there much longer, the enemy would have picked us all off. I saw this, and begged Colonel Nesbitt of the 47th to form on our left, in order that we might advance with our bayonets to the parapet. I ran from right to left, and stopped our men from firing; while this was doing, and when we had got in tolerable order, we rushed on, leaped the ditch, and climbed the parapet, under a most sore and heavy fire.

There was a moment at the last when the British staggered once again—a moment when the battle's outcome hung in the balance—then they recovered and came on with a rush. Prescott said later that one more round of ammunition might have pushed them back then and there, but there was not one more round. The last American volley sputtered out "like an old candle," and with a great animal roar that was heard in Boston the redcoats surged forward. Bayonets glinted in the smoky gloom, the mitered hats of the big grenadiers loomed over the breastwork. Angry, sweating redcoats, the breath sobbing in their throats, stormed up the dirt walls of the redoubt as the marines poured in from the right. All the pent-up anger and misery and frustration of that ghastly afternoon was in their charge, and there was no stopping them. They had murder in their eyes, and they lashed out, stabbing and slashing with the bayonet, not bothering to fire, cursing, yelling, pressing the assault home with the terrible brutal fury of which man is sometimes capable.

Almost none of the Americans had bayonets—nothing but clubbed muskets or fists or rocks—yet they fought, one regular said, "more like Devils than Men" in this hand-to-hand melee. Even so, Prescott saw there was no chance and ordered his men to retreat, to get out as best they could. Peter Brown was "not suffered to be toutched, altho' I was in the fort when the Enemy came in, and jumped over the walls, and ran half a mile where Balls flew like Hailstones, and Canons roared like Thunder."

Captain Ebenezer Bancroft had just taken the ramrod from his firelock when a British officer leaped at him. He fired, killing the man, then rushed for the entrance to the redoubt, holding his gun "broadwise before my face" to keep from being clubbed. A rifle butt smashed down on his shoulder, and as he ran toward Bunker Hill, weak with fatigue, sightless in one eye, he realized that the forefinger of his left hand was gone. Coffee Whittemore, a Negro, had a hole in

his hat from a musket ball, and in the final moments of the fight he seized a sword from a fallen British officer and carried it off in triumph (to the disgust of his friends, he sold it a few days later).

Amos Farnsworth was another who stayed in the redoubt until the enemy broke through, and when the retreat began he raced out about ten or fifteen rods past the outlet, where he "received a wound in my rite arm, the bawl gowing through a little below my elbow breaking the little shel bone. Another bawl struck my back, taking a piece of skin about as big as a penny. But I got to Cambridge that night." Colonel Ebenezer Bridge had his head and neck laid open by a British sword. His second-in-command, Moses Parker, was groveling in the dirt, one knee fractured by a ball; but it was every man for himself in these frantic closing moments of the fight, and Parker was left behind, to be taken prisoner and to die after a British surgeon amputated his leg.

The redoubt that had protected Prescott's troops all day nearly became a death-trap for them now. There was only one narrow exit at the rear of the fort, and the black smoke and dust were so thick the men had to feel their way along the walls to find it. Yet this weird gloom kept the uneven struggle from becoming a massacre; the British could not tell friend from foe and dared not fire into the mass of men crowded around the passage. It was a nightmare of confusion and chaos, with the shadowy figures of wildly shouting, moving men, half-panicked as they surged and fought their way toward the only exit, half-mad with rage as they beat off the thrust of death from behind. Prescott refused to run; striding toward the opening with sword raised, he parried the swipes of bayonets, and although his coat and waistcoat were pierced, he was not injured.

When he and the other Americans emerged from the fort, they found themselves between two approaching bodies of the enemy which had enveloped the redoubt from opposite sides, and while neither of these could fire for fear of hitting their own men, other British were coming up from behind, scaling the rear wall of the redoubt, shooting into the retreating rebels. Prescott's adjutant went down, and Captains Maxwell, Dow, and Farwell were wounded.

Somewhere, in the last wild rush, Joseph Warren disappeared in the murk of battle. The man Lord Rawdon called "the greatest incendiary in all America," who had once said he would like to die fighting the British in blood up to his knees, got his wish. No one saw him fall, but he was hit in the head by a ball and must have been killed instantly. "He died in his best cloaths," a British officer wrote; "everybody remembers his fine silk-fringed waistcoat."

All resistance in the redoubt and the breastwork collapsed at last, but fortunately for those who were fleeing, the rail fence held firm and the defenders there were able to cover their comrades' retreat before withdrawing themselves in good order. A handful of fresh men led by William Coit and John Chester kept up a "brisk fire" from behind a stone wall along the way, and some thirty of Stark's men helped Samuel Trevett bring off one of his fieldpieces—the only one the rebels managed to save. They succeeded in hauling it to the summit of Bunker Hill before a British company sighted the prize and stormed after them, and there was a rough little encounter, with several American losses, before Trevett and the New Hampshiremen drove off the attackers and dragged the gun away.

The entire American left flank, acting as a rear guard, fell back stubbornly, carrying their wounded with them, taking cover wherever they found it, and returning the British fire like professional troops. The last rebels to leave were those with the most to fight for—the Charlestown company of Thomas Gardner's regiment, who had hurried into line at the rail fence just before the third British attack. They had lost their colonel (Gardner was mortally wounded while trying to lead reinforcements to the redoubt, and was carried off the field on a litter of rails by his son and some other men); they had watched, helpless, while their village and their homes went up in flames; and if ever a company was fighting mad, it was this one. But there was nothing much that anyone could do now, beyond saving his own skin.

Fortunately for the Americans, the British had very nearly reached the end of their string. They had climbed Breed's Hill three times that afternoon, and the grisly slopes were littered with their dead; twice victory had eluded them, and when it came at last it was because discipline and courage overcame fear and exhaustion and defeat. By all rights these men had been beaten; now they were utterly worn out by their efforts, their losses were staggering, their morale was nearly gone, and if they paused to draw breath and failed to pursue the still contentious Americans, it was no wonder.

Some of the best of them were gone. Colonel James Abercromby, the commander of the grenadiers, was dying; so was Major Pitcairn of the marines, who had been carried back to Boston by his son. Someone who saw the younger man, covered with blood, wandering dazedly through the streets of the town, was about to help him when he was informed that the blood was from the father's wound. Gage sent a doctor immediately to Pitcairn, but the marine knew he was dying and refused to let the physician waste his time. To young Jeremy Lister fell the task of telling Lieutenant Kelley's wife of her husband's mortal wound and of standing by helplessly while she "for some time sat motionless with two small Children close by her."

Henry Clinton arrived at the scene of victory at the moment when Howe, seeing as if for the first time the number of British dead on the field, was beginning to realize its cost. Not one of the General's aides was left; all were either killed or wounded. The pride of the army, the flank companies, had been cut to ribbons, and the toll of officers and men in all regiments was appalling. When Clinton saw him, Howe was far from a victorious general; he was exhausted, his white gaiters streaked with blood from the long grass on the hill, and he had the look of a man who has stared death and disaster in the face.

Howe admitted privately to Clinton that his left "was totally gone" just before the final onslaught, and Clinton was so disturbed by all he saw and heard during these few moments that he committed his impressions to cipher: "All was in Confusion, officers told me that they could not command their men and I never saw so great a want of order."

But if Howe, undone by the battle, wanted energy, Clinton did not. He saw at once that the rebels must be driven off the peninsula while they were still disorganized, and after stationing a detachment of 100 men in Prescott's abandoned redoubt, he took all the able-bodied troops that were available, caught up with Pigot, who had already moved after the Americans, and headed up the road to Bunker Hill. Off to his right, Stark and Knowlton and Gardner were still making their way deliberately and obstinately toward the rear, their men putting up "a running fight," Lord Rawdon wrote admiringly, "from one fence, or wall, to another."

Burgoyne, too, complimented the rebels on their retreat. It was, he said, "no flight: it was even covered with bravery and military skill." (They were so successful in bringing off their wounded that the British took only thirty-one prisoners, most of them mortally injured.) Despite the sudden collapse of their defenses and the precipitous retreat from the redoubt, the Provincials simply refused to give up.

A few diehards were even firing from the remains of houses around Charlestown (Clinton was annoyed from that direction while he proceeded down the middle of the peninsula), but the end was in sight. Clinton, expecting the rebels to make a stand on the back side of Bunker Hill, was amazed to find it deserted; he posted a force there, sent skirmishers out to man the stone walls between this point and the Neck, and satisfying himself that the enemy was being vigorously pressed, returned to Boston.

Just as in the redoubt, the Americans paid dearly for having left themselves but one narrow avenue of retreat. To make an orderly withdrawal under fire from a losing field was too much to expect under the best of circumstances, but when more than a thousand frantic, disorganized troops, heading for the safety of the mainland, were suddenly compressed into a solid mass to funnel across the Neck, which was only about thirty-five yards wide at its narrowest point, the result was chaos.

Progress was impeded by the wounded and by the debris of battle; British musket fire was closing in from the rear; and to make matters far worse, the entire Neck was being raked by the guns of the *Glasgow.* One thought was uppermost in the mind of everyone, and that was to reach the other side as quickly as possible. Desperately they surged forward, pushing and shoving, stumbling and falling over wounded men and pieces of men blown apart by the merciless British cannon, shouting in anger and terror and frustration as they fought to get out of this trap.

Thirty-six hours ago they had last rested; they had been a full day without food or water; and for men totally unused to war and unprepared, they had seen it all—continuous pounding from enemy cannon, frontal assaults by veteran infantry, the shattering climax of a bayonet charge and hand-to-hand combat. Already driven beyond the limits of human endurance, they were forced to call forth some final reserve of energy, and incredibly they did so, to make this frenzied dash across the confining causeway.

Once the solid artery of retreat hit the wider reaches of the mainland it broke up into little groups that scattered across the moors and clay pits of Charlestown Common, moving inland toward a sinking sun. Utterly spent, some of the Provincials did not even bother to look back; their only thought was of camp and rest and a security that had seemed impossible minutes before. And as they disappeared, straggling off along the dusty roads toward Cambridge and Medford, the battle for Bunker Hill was over, except for one last incident.

It must have been after 5:30 P.M., when the *Somerset* log reported that the "firing slackened," that Major Andrew McClary, of Stark's regiment, reached the mainland. Looking back, he saw Clinton's detachment

moving onto the crest of Bunker Hill, and just to make certain that they had no plans to push on toward the mainland, he recrossed the Neck, went close enough to the British lines to decide that no further attack was intended, and finally headed back to rejoin his command. Walking alone in the gathering dusk, he had almost reached safety when a last cannon ball from the *Glasgow* tore him to pieces. As a historian wrote long afterward, "No smaller weapon seemed worthy to destroy the gigantic hero."

Back in Boston, the impatient Clinton had turned his thoughts to a counterstroke, to be delivered immediately. Such was "the Panick" in the rebel ranks, he thought, that a thousand men could easily sweep up their entire defenses. But the Americans, to their everlasting credit, were already at work digging again, fortifying Winter Hill on the mainland side of Charlestown Neck, where, as Lieutenant Colonel Experience Storrs recorded in his diary, "We immediately went to entrenching; flung up by morning an entrenchment 100 feet square. Done principally by our regiment under Putnam's directions, had but little sleep the night."

Henry Clinton should have known better. No one wrote a better epitaph on the battle than he did that evening, nor gave a more convincing reason for not resuming it: "A dear bought victory, another such would have ruined us."

For the British, the victory was costly beyond its worth. Nearly one-half of Howe's 2,300 men were casualties: 226 had been killed and 828 wounded, a total of 1,054. Though the Americans had suffered much less heavily—of the estimated 3,500 men who had seen action that day, perhaps 450 had been shot—their situation was precarious. There is every likelihood that if the British had pursued their advantage, the Provincial army might have been destroyed. But as the days stretched into weeks, and the weeks into months, the British dallied. In October, Gage was relieved of his command and replaced by Howe—who felt that nothing would be lost by waiting until spring to settle accounts with the besieging rebels. Once again a British commander had failed to reckon on the determination of the Americans. In the dead of winter, they brought forty-three cannon and sixteen mortars cross-country from Fort Ticonderoga; suddenly the fate of Boston was sealed. On the night of March 2, 1776, the army—now led by George Washington—seized the strategic heights at Dorchester. Howe was left with but two alternatives—to risk another Bunker Hill or to evacuate the town. By now a thoroughly chastened man, he chose the latter.

"My beloved and good Husband . . ."

CONTINUED FROM PAGE 27

to. "Cheer up thy heart in expectation of God's goodness to us," she wrote; "Let nothing dismay or discourage thee. If the Lord be with us, who can be against us?"

Events moved fast. The decision for New England made, John made contact with a group of Puritans who would sail with him. Within weeks of the loss of his court position in June of 1629, he was in conference with the emigrating group; within four months he was named governor of the company, which was to depart in the spring of 1630; within a year—after feverish months of gathering ships, settlers, supplies, and equipment—he sailed. To Margaret he wrote in good-by:

And now (my sweet soul) I must once again take my last farewell of thee in old England. It goeth very near to my heart to leave thee, but I know to whom I have committed thee, even to Him who loves thee much better than any husband can.

On his last visit to Groton before sailing, he and Margaret had arranged to set aside a time each week when, if they could not write, they could think of each other. Now he reminded her:

When I shall be at some leisure, I shall not avoid the remembrance of thee, nor the grief for thy absence. Thou hast thy share with me, but I hope the course we have agreed upon will be some ease to us both. Mondays and Fridays, at five of the clock at night, we shall meet in spirit, till we meet in person. . . .

Only the younger children remained at Groton with Margaret as she waited—pregnant again and troubled by tenants who, with the master gone and depression abroad, were recalcitrant about the rents—for word from America. John's voyage to Massachusetts Bay would take three months, she might have figured; the return of a ship, another three. She could not expect a letter for half a year.

As she waited, thirty-nine now and no longer young, she spent her time preparing to leave Groton where she had been a bride and the east country of England where she had been a girl. Undoubtedly she met John "in spirit" each Monday and Friday. Undoubtedly, too, she read and reread the pamphlets on New England John had left her. Certainly she lacked nothing, for John had given her brother, Deane Tyndal, fifteen hundred pounds to be invested should anything happen to him. Then, finally, a letter came, bringing news welcome and unwelcome. John himself was well and happy, the New World countryside was better than they had expected, but Henry—"my son Henry,

my son Henry, ah, poor child!"—had drowned. Other news came, some telling of hardships, hunger, and disease during the first winter in Massachusetts. But from John: "Be not discouraged (my dear wife) by anything thou shalt hear from hence, for I see no cause to repent our coming hither." Margaret must join him soon, he wrote, and the greater part of his letters detailed the supplies and equipment that she should bring with her: "Two or three skillets of several sizes, and a large frying pan . . . store of linen for use at sea, and sack to bestow among the sailors; some drinking vessels, and pewter . . . And for phisick you shall need no other but a pound of Doctor Wright's *Electuarium Lenitium,* and his direction to use it."

With John's letters to encourage and guide her, Margaret hurried preparations for her own departure, urging her stepson, John, Jr., to make haste in selling Groton Manor and arranging passage. "My heart and thoughts are there already," she wrote to him from London. "I want but means to carry my body after them." Her brother advised her to wait awhile, but as she wrote young John, "I hope to break through that, and get his good will. . . . Therefore, my good son, let me intreat thee to take order for our going as soon as thou canst." Brother Deane was won over—who could refuse Margaret?—and in the summer of 1631 she sailed on the ship *Lyon.* With her went John, Jr., his family, and the other children, including the daughter John had never seen and never would. The new baby, Anne, died, and was buried at sea. In November, the ship entered Massachusetts Bay, and Margaret's arrival set off a celebration. Squire John had fallen in love with the paraphernalia of power, and now he spread them before his beloved wife. As Margaret was rowed ashore, the harbor reverberated with a "six or seven gun" salute from ships lying at anchor. On the beach the infant colony's military might, "the captains with their companions in arms," volleyed and paraded past. Feasting followed—"fat hogs, kid, venison, poultry, geese, partridges"—and her husband, the governor, proclaimed November 11 a day of thanksgiving—for the harvest, the prosperity of the colony, and his wife's arrival.

The Boston that Margaret came to was but a poor, straggling settlement set on a rolling, grass-covered peninsula jutting out into Massachusetts Bay. Its houses were for the most part wigwamlike huts of thatch, linked together by winding footpaths. Anticipating Margaret's arrival, John had hurried the construction of a frame house, but it was probably unfinished when she landed—Governor William Bradford of nearby Plymouth Colony, their first guest, stayed aboard a ship in the bay. In the early 1640's they would move into another house, one with six rooms, elaborate for a wilderness. The craftsmanship was of the crudest, and all Margaret's womanliness was needed to make the bare walls a home. Even so, the house was plain and sparsely furnished, the hall (or living room) never boasting more than a cupboard, six chairs, a table, a white notions box, a case of bottles (wine from Madeira was commonly drunk in the family), pewter and tin plates, candlestands, snuffers, and here and there a piece of bric-a-brac, remembrances of Groton. John's "study" with its books and writing materials—where every day, in the words of a contemporary, he wrote "particular passages of the country in a great book" (his journal *History of New England*) —did duty as workshop and armory too. Yet for Margaret, John was there, John who had written during their separation: "Oh, how it refresheth my heart to think that I shall yet again see thy sweet face in the land of the living; that lovely countenance that I have so much delighted in and beheld with so great content."

If it straggled in 1631, Boston and the colony grew quickly. During the first ten years some fifteen thousand people landed at Boston and spread out to settle as far as the Merrimack River in the northeast and the Connecticut in the southwest. Boston itself boasted well over one thousand people by 1640. Paths became streets; a new meetinghouse was built, and a market; substantial frame houses—John Coddington built the first brick house—each set in its own garden plot, gave the settlement the look of a village, then a town. One center of life was the church, and every Sabbath a bell called the Winthrops and their neighbors to prayer and preaching. The other center was Margaret's house, for during most of his life in Massachusetts John

served as governor. During regular sessions of the General Court, Massachusetts' legislature, liveried militiamen formed a governor's guard at the house; leading freemen and deputies crowded the "hall" and spilled over into the side parlor, which did double duty as bedroom for the master and mistress. Even between sessions the house was host to the great and near-great of the colony and the Puritan world outside—John Cotton, Sir Harry Vane, Roger Williams, Hugh Peter, Bradford of Plymouth, Thomas Hooker of Connecticut, Saltonstalls, Bradstreets, Dudleys, big and bluff John Endecott. This constant flurry of visitors, at least, was familiar to Margaret from Groton Manor.

She had much to learn and unlearn now. Even Thomas Tusser's *Huswiferie* hints would have failed her, for Tusser and England knew nothing of the Indian corn that replaced wheat as a staple food; nothing of cooking without an abundance of expensive spices; nothing of silk grass, which replaced hemp and flax for the first few years, or of milkweed, which supplied candlewicks and filled pillows and bolsters. Yet Margaret had help in adapting to her new surroundings; some of the Groton servants had come over with John and gained a year's experience which they passed on to their mistress. And if there were differences, there were many similarities between life in America and life in England. Unlike later American frontiers, this first one relied heavily on what it could buy from "home." Margaret's clothes, her linens, her "best" candles, her utensils; John's books and swords and guns and tools; the equipment and livestock for the farms surrounding the town—all were brought in by ship. The colony was a "little England," somewhat coarser and much simplified.

In Massachusetts, John was regularly at home, and this was a difference between the colony and Groton that Margaret found most pleasant. As governor or magistrate, John was ever busy with the daily business

A romanticized nineteenth-century etching depicts John Winthrop's arrival in Massachusetts in 1630.

of government—to the neglect of his own affairs and the resultant diminution of his once-substantial income—and he was often perplexed by the sharp controversies that constantly broke out in the Puritan commonwealth. But at night he would come home to Margaret, to his books, and to his carpenter's bench—he had turned out to be a quite respectable carpenter. Only occasionally did he have to travel, and then it was within the comparatively narrow confines of the colony. Few letters of the last years remain. Probably few were written, there being no postal system and not many travelers to carry a hurried note from Ipswich or Salem to Boston and Margaret:

My sweet wife: . . . I praise God I am well. The Lord bless thee and all ours. So I kiss thee a second time. Farewell. . . .

I was unwillingly hindered from coming to thee, nor am I like to see thee before the last day of this week. . . . The Lord bless and keep thee, my sweet wife, and all our family, and send us a comfortable meeting. So I kiss thee and love thee ever. . . .

I am still detained from thee, but it is by the Lord who hath a greater interest in me than thyself. When this work is done He will restore me to thee again, to our mutual comfort, Amen. I thank thee for thy sweet letter; my heart was with thee to have written to thee every day, but business would not permit me. . . .

And one from Margaret, dated 1637 and bearing a mark of sadness engendered by a religious schism which was then dividing the colony into two bitter and irreconcilable groups:

Dear in my thoughts, I blush to think how much I have neglected the opportunity of presenting my love to you. Sad thoughts possess my spirits, and I cannot repulse them, which makes me unfit for anything, wondering what the Lord means by all these troubles among us. . . .

Again the years pass. In 1640 John was fifty-two, Margaret forty-nine, old age for that era. Past troubles subsided—recalcitrant Indians were destroyed in war; the religious schismatics were expelled—and new ones arose. In the early 1640's, the colony was threatened by French invasion; controversy arose with the Dutch at New Netherlands; Puritan revolt broke out in England, and many Massachusetts leaders returned to fight in the war that followed, some to vote for the decapitation of Charles I. Even John thought of returning, but decided his work lay in New England. In 1645 a quarrel within Massachusetts saw John impeached but then acquitted. Children died, including all of Margaret's stepchildren but young John. The four of her own who had grown to manhood remained, though: Stephen, who was to sit in Cromwell's Parliament; Adam; Deane; and Samuel, who later became governor of Antigua in the West Indies. And despite tribulation

in the colony, the Puritan commonwealth was, to Margaret, a sanctuary: "When I think of the troublesome times and manifold distractions . . ." she wrote to John, Jr., who was in England at the time, "I think we do not prize our happiness here as we have cause, that we should be in peace when so many troubles are in most places of the world. I wish we were more sensible of the calamities of others . . ."

In the summer of 1647, as John began his eleventh term as governor of the colony, an "epidemical sickness" broke out among the Indians and spread to the settlers. Forty died, and one of them was Margaret, who came down with the sickness on the afternoon of June 13 and was dead the next morning. The husband she had bolstered, cheered, and loved mourned her but went quietly about his work as governor—a new Indian crisis was impending. In his journal he noted only that she "left this world for a better, being about fifty-six years of age, a woman of singular virtue, prudence, modesty, and piety, and specially beloved and honored of all the country." The following year, the loneliness unbearable, he married again, taking to wife Mistress Martha Coytemore, a widow. Less than a year later—on March 26, 1649—he too died.

Long before, as they had parted, one to travel to Massachusetts and the other to wait at Groton, John had written to Margaret of their eventual reunion: "Yet, if all these hopes should fail, blessed be our God that we are assured we shall meet one day, if not as husband and wife, yet in a better condition. Let that stay and comfort thy heart."

Darrett B. Rutman, assistant professor of Early American History at the University of Minnesota, is currently at work on a book about Boston during John Winthrop's lifetime.

For further reading: The Puritan Dilemma: The Story of John Winthrop, *by Edmund S. Morgan (Little, Brown, 1958).*

Yet eventually the Blaine story was sold to a newspaper by the man who had brought it to Cleveland. It disclosed that Mrs. Blaine had borne her first child hardly three months after the recorded date of their marriage. Blaine's enemies leaped on the news, even making dramatic use of the pathetic detail that the birth date on the tombstone of the child had been defaced. The Democratic *Sentinel,* in Indianapolis, where bank failures from a country-wide economic slowdown were roiling tempers, exploited the scandal viciously:

There is hardly an intelligent man in the country who has not heard that James G. Blaine betrayed the girl whom he married, and then only married her at the muzzle of a shotgun . . . if, after despoiling her, he was the craven to refuse her legal redress, giving legitimacy to her child, until a loaded shotgun stimulated his conscience—then there is a blot on his character more foul, if possible, than any of the countless stains on his political record.

Blaine noisily brought suit against the *Sentinel,* and rushed into print with an elaborate rebuttal. He claimed that there had been *two* marriage ceremonies. In 1850, he said, he was twenty years old, living in Kentucky, engaged to the woman who would be his wife, when,

I was suddenly summoned to Pennsylvania by the death of my father. It being very doubtful if I could return to Kentucky, I was threatened with an indefinite separation from her who possessed my entire devotion. My one wish was to secure her to myself by an indissoluble tie against every possible contingency in life, and, on the 30th day of June, 1850, just prior to my departure from Kentucky, we were, in the presence of my trusted and chosen friends, united by what I knew was, in my native state of Pennsylvania, a perfectly legal form of marriage.

A second marriage was performed some six months later, in March, in Pennsylvania, but the date was kept secret "for obvious reasons." Three months more, and the child was born.

Blaine's married life had been long and honorable, and he might better have said bluntly, as Cleveland did, "Tell the truth." Blaine's many critics saw the evasions in his rebuttal and wrote copiously about them to the newspapers. Why keep the first marriage secret until his wife was six months pregnant? Why the vague details about the first wedding? Who were the witnesses? Why was there no record? Lawyers discussed the laws of Kentucky and Pennsylvania, to Blaine's disadvantage. The newspapers sporadically kept the story alive, but it never became an important issue, partly because Cleveland spurned it, but mainly because it was lost in the furious clamor over Blaine's public immorality.

Probably no presidential candidate ever made himself more vulnerable to attack than Blaine. There was little that was positive to say about his long record as Speaker and senator, except for his pretentious patriotism; he had sponsored no significant legislation, and his tenure as Garfield's Secretary of State had been brief. But on the negative side there was much to say, particularly about his association with profiteers and influence-buying railroad promoters: men disliked him for the friends he made. And none disliked him more than some elements in his own party. His Half-Breeds of course supported him, as did many of the Stalwarts, since for most of the spoilsmen any Republican was better than none—though when Blaine's old enemy Roscoe Conkling was asked to make a speech defending the "plumed knight," his bitter refusal became famous: "You know I don't engage in criminal practice." A great majority of the Mugwumps, who had been fighting so long for honest Republicanism, could not stomach Blaine. They pledged themselves to the Democrat.

The snarling Republican civil war that followed was even more bitter than that between the two parties. Die-hard Republicans snubbed their Independent friends, and moved their church pews to avoid contact. Leading Mugwump journals had given fair warning: before the nominating convention the *New York Times* had said it would not support Blaine, and *Harper's Weekly* had strongly opposed him; but the acrimony heaped on them, and on other Republican papers that joined the attack, was angry and threatening. *Harper's Weekly* lost thousands of dollars in revenue, and its editor, George William Curtis, and Thomas Nast, its crusading cartoonist, were assailed in the die-hard press and dropped by personal friends. They stood firm; Nast the more so because, in the economic depression lowering over the country, his savings were swept away when ex-President Grant's brokerage firm, as badly mismanaged as Grant's administration, fell to pieces, bringing ruin to many who had believed in the old war hero, and bewilderment and disillusion to Grant himself ("I don't see," he said, "how I can ever trust any human being again"). Inevitably the nation was reminded of the old scandals, and of Blaine's profiteering.

Now a startling disclosure rocked the campaign. Mulligan released additional Blaine-Fisher letters, and the Plumed Knight was nakedly exposed. The corre-

POLLS

Leslie's Illustrated, *in this postelection cartoon, showed "the silent vote" veering toward Cleveland, with Benjamin F. Butler, who had sought the labor vote on two minor tickets, completely bottled up by unfortunate political support.*

spondence, widely printed in full for all to see, made it obvious that when Blaine had bared his soul before the House and the country, he had systematically lied and equivocated. But this was not the worst of it. The letters showed Blaine servilely begging, on the basis of his political influence, for a large share of the Little Rock Railroad securities.

In one early note, pleading for his share in the railroad, the House Speaker urged, "I do not feel that I shall prove a dead-head in this enterprise if I once embark on it. I see various channels in which I know I can be useful." An offer is made to him, and he fawns on Fisher: "Your liberal mode of dealing with me . . . had not passed without my full appreciation." He sends Fisher a copy of the Congressional Record showing how serviceable to the railroad one of his House rulings has been. Next Blaine suggests how useful he can be to Fisher and his friends if they want to take advantage of National Bank expansion and start a bank in Little Rock. "It will be to some extent a matter of favoritism as to who gets the banks . . . and it will be in my power to 'cast an anchor to windward' in your behalf if you desire it. . ."

In 1876, with congressional investigation—and the presidential nomination—imminent, Blaine grows full of urgency and anxiety, "Certain papers and persons are trying to throw mud at me to injure my candidacy before the Cincinnati convention . . ." he writes Fisher. "I want you to send me a letter such as the enclosed draft . . . Regard this letter as strictly confidential. Do not show it to anyone." And then the immortal ending: "Kind regards to Mrs. Fisher. Burn this letter." There follows, for Fisher to copy, an "unsolicited" testimonial addressed to Blaine about Blaine's lily-white innocence in the business: "The transaction was perfectly open, and there was no more secrecy in regard to it than if you had been buying flour or sugar . . . your action in the whole matter was as open and fair as day."

Faced with the printed correspondence, which Blaine could not deny was his, the die-hard Republicans carefully avoided discussing the details, and argued that Blaine had only been engaged in a normal commercial transaction; any businessman might have done the same. The exchange between Senator George Hoar, of Massachusetts, a Blaine partisan, and Carl Schurz, the great Mugwump, was representative. "The purity of the American home," said Hoar, "without which there can be no purity or health anywhere, is safer with those who are trying to extirpate Mormonism than with those in whose eyes Grover Cleveland is the standard of personal excellence." Schurz asked why Blaine, in 1876, had not opened all his records and the correspondence to the full view of investigators. Hoar's answer was lame: The circumstances were dangerous, party feeling was high, Blaine felt "inexpressibly outraged and indignant" at having his correspondence examined by a hostile, Democratic congressional committee. George Washington himself would have been indignant, Hoar suggested.

Schurz was sure no "Mulligan letters" would have been found in Washington's correspondence, but he enjoyed imagining what such a letter might have been like:

Headquarters of the Continental Army
T. W. Fisher, *Esq., Army Contractor*
My dear Mr. Fisher: Your offer to admit me to participation in your beef contract is very generous. Accept my thanks. But I want more. You spoke of your friend Caldwell, who has a flour contract, as willing to dispose of a share of his interest to me. I wish he would make the proposition definite. Tell him that I feel I shall not prove a deadhead in the enterprise. I see various channels in which I know I can be useful.

Sincerely your friend,
George Washington

A loud band of Democrats and anti-Blaine Republicans was less subtle than Schurz. In print, in posters, and in street songs they continuously reminded the

Plumed Knight of the servile phrases of his correspondence. They discovered fresh evidence of other profiteering in railroads. Blaine was handled with particular roughness in New York. As the campaign wore on, it became clear that New York's thirty-six electoral votes would decide the election; and there the intensity of feeling about Cleveland's morality, the concentration in the state of leading Mugwump spokesmen, plus the angry press rivalries, turned the campaign into a political circus.

Nast led the cartoonists in savagely lampooning Blaine. His cartooned Blaine had a coarse face reminiscent of Boss Tweed's—and indeed, Nast would bring back the ghost of the old Democratic boss and confront the two, to underline the resemblance. Blaine was usually shown with a top hat, bearing three white plumes that grew steadily the worse for wear; then a perspiring, evasive Blaine substituted for the plumes a feather clearly labeled "white," and became "the knight of the white feather." Blaine's famous letters were remembered: Slippery Jim was seen dictating his alibi to Fisher, and Jay Gould, the monster tycoon, assures him, "I see many channels in which you could be useful, my dear knight." Gould was known as the great dispenser of "soap"—money used to buy votes—and Nast carefully kept alive his association with Blaine. The humor magazines made great sport of Slippery Jim. In massive two-page color cartoons in *Puck* he was eternally a sad-faced, hapless circus clown tattooed with the legends of his scandals—hence the parade cry *"Jim! Jim! Tat-tooed Jim!"*

It was in the street parades that the enthusiasm and anger of both sides found their most spectacular outlet. Costumes cost from 50 cents to $150, and came in all colors and designs: all-out Blaine enthusiasts even marched in knightly suits of armor. The *Tribune* noted approvingly the high tone of Blaine parades in New York: "There were no newly-arrived immigrants in line, as was the case in the Cleveland parade." Broadway was jammed, and "omnibuses threading their way slowly through the mass of human beings, were almost lifted from the ground." The Republicans occasionally lightened their march with such calls as *"Ma, Ma, where's my Pa?"* but their chief campaign cry, chanted for hours, was *"Blaine! Blaine! James G. Blaine!"* often with the rhyme, *"The white plumed knight from the state of Maine!"*

The Democrats hooted back: *"Blaine! Blaine! Jay Gould Blaine! The Continental Liar from the state of Maine!"*

The Democrats had the best of it, because they had more ammunition. Banners and pantomimes mocked Blaine's letters, most effectively of all in a great Cleveland citizens' march up Broadway the last week of the campaign. Fired-up partisans walked for three hours "in the muddy street," some 30,000 of them—the "Greatest Parade in New York's History," the partisan *Times* reported. Broadway was waiting for them. Number 618 was "decorated with a great canvas picture that stretched across the entire front of the building, representing Mr. Fisher hesitating before a lighted candle with Mr. Blaine's fatal letter."

The campaign was hard on Blaine. In October, a New York *Herald* correspondent described his "harried and drawn face, blanched to a degree of pallor that was startling." But as he swung back from a western speaking tour at the end of the month, weary and harassed by the chanted reminders of his follies, he had yet the assurance that he was winning. The South and some northern states would go for Cleveland; but there was enough die-hard Republican strength in the North, enough Republican "soap" to outweigh Democratic "soap," enough reaction to the "immoralities" of Cleveland, to put Blaine in. The public profligate was proving more acceptable than the private one. All Blaine had to make sure of was New York; and the Republicans openly, and some Democrats privately, were giving him the state.

Nevertheless, he engaged in two ambitious moves to nail down New York's votes. One was a banquet in his honor at Delmonico's, with Jay Gould hovering in the background. The object was to introduce Blaine to the assembled commercial wealth of New York, to present him as the "businessman's candidate," and to get financial support for the final drive of the campaign. It was a great sybaritic dinner with the best food and drink, and Blaine ornamented it with a speech on Republican prosperity and the dangers of Democratic meddling; but the meal left a bad taste. Blaine was unhappy at the poor return in contributions—Gould's rich friends could not be stampeded into generosity by fear of Cleveland—and Blaine's enemies were furious at the conspicuous extravagance of the affair in a time of depressed national economy. The *World* found a descriptive phrase that stuck: "Belshazzar's Feast."

Bad as the banquet was for Blaine, his other involvement on that fateful October week was even worse. As a result of a single remark, he was caught in the Catholic controversy almost before he knew what was happening. To be either too strongly pro-Catholic or anti-Catholic was dangerous then, with the influx of new Irish voters. Cleveland had been accused of being anti-Irish and anti-Catholic (as well as pro-Mormon—Utah's polygamy being a live issue, as Senator Hoar's attack indicates). By walking carefully between Catholic and anti-Catholic abysses, Blaine had reached the campaign's last week uncommitted religiously, despite the fact that his mother and sisters were Catholics. On that October 29, it seemed a good and harmless idea for him to meet with a large delegation of friendly ministers, to emphasize his "moral" acceptability as opposed to that of the philanderer Cleveland. Blaine needed an easy, undemanding meeting; he was very tired now. Hence a then-prominent religious orator, a certain Dr. Tiffany, was simply to deliver an elegant congratulation on Blaine's assured election.

Then a little thing went wrong. Some of the ministers objected, with considerable feeling, to Tiffany's being singled out for the main speech. Why Tiffany? The matter was settled in what seemed a harmless way: Samuel D. Burchard, the oldest parson present, would speak first. Dr. Burchard was known to be an anti-Catholic, but certainly he would not use this meeting to speak out his feelings; after all, Blaine, on his way to New York, had visited the convent in Indiana where his sister was Mother Superior.

Weary Blaine, trying to think out what *he* would say, did not quite listen to Burchard. He might better have listened. Buried in the parson's assurances that these friends would never desert him was one of the immortal phrases of American campaign history: "We are Republicans and don't propose to leave our party and identify ourselves with the party whose antecedents have been rum, Romanism and rebellion."

Rum, Romanism, and rebellion! . . . Blaine did not hear; but a Democrat did. It was, in fact, a scout from Cleveland headquarters, which was only a short distance away. Cleveland's good friend William Hudson was at headquarters that night, and he graphically described the scene later:

> . . . we heard some one come up the stairs in great haste. In a moment Colonel John Tracey, the head of the newspaper bureau, plunged into the room so much out of breath by reason of his haste and excitement that he could not speak—could only point to pages of paper he had. Gorman [Democratic senator from Maryland] took the papers from his hand, and on reading the words pointed out straightened up with a start and earnestly read the context. The words pointed out were "Rum, Romanism and Rebellion! . . ."
>
> "Surely," said Gorman sternly, "Blaine met this remark?"
>
> "That is the astounding thing," said Tracey excitedly. "He made no reference to the words. I have confirmed that fact. . ."
>
> Finally Senator Gorman spoke, his voice cracking like the snap of a whip:
>
> "This sentence must be in every daily newspaper in the country tomorrow, no matter how, no matter what it costs. Organize for that immediately, Colonel Tracey, and it must be kept alive for the rest of the campaign. . ."

The next day Blaine became conscious of the terrible mistake, and tried desperately to disassociate him-

Rain failed to wet down the enthusiasm of anyone (possibly excepting the streetcar horses) as the election returns were released in New York. The scene opposite is Printing House Square, at the intersection of Park Row and Nassau Street.

self from Burchard's notorious alliteration—but it was too late. Gorman hammered it at the Irish and at other Catholic groups, especially in their New York and New England strongholds. They turned angry.

On the next Tuesday, November 4, all Blaine's enemies rose against him—the Democrats, the Mugwumps, the independent citizens shocked by his profligacy in office, the disillusioned Irish and other Catholics. Still, the current ran strong against Cleveland, the honest, private profligate: when the votes were in, the Democrats won New York by a bare 1,149 votes out of more than 1,100,000 cast—and New York, as prophesied, made the difference in the election. Over the nation, with some ten million votes cast, Cleveland defeated Blaine by less than 63,000. Public and private morality had run almost a dead heat.

Relieved Democrats, in their victory celebrations, could chant forgivingly: *"Hurray for Maria! Hurray for the kid! I voted for Cleveland, and I'm damned glad I did!"*

It wasn't so easy for Cleveland. He would carry the wounds of this campaign; and even after he went into the White House, even after he married in 1886, gossip would follow him. He had come into politics almost unwillingly thus far, and he wrote to his friend Wilson Bissell, "I look upon the four years next to come as a dreadful self-inflicted penance for the good of my country. I can see no pleasure in it and no satisfaction, only a hope that I may be of service to my people." He asks when he can safely visit Buffalo, the home town that had believed the scandal thrown at him and given its vote to Blaine, and then he concludes sadly, "Elected President of the United States, I feel I have no home *at my home.*"

Said his campaign companion and good friend Lamont, "Cleveland was never the same man after that awful campaign of '84. I think he was bigger and broader. But—he was never the same man."

Marvin Rosenberg is a professor of dramatic art at the University of California, Berkeley. During World War II, he served as a senior editor with the Office of War Information, and later directed a section of the State Department's International Broadcasting Division. He has published a book on Shakespeare's Othello, *entitled* The Masks of Othello. *His wife, Dorothy, is a free-lance writer whose work has appeared in such publications as the* Saturday Review.

For further reading: Grover Cleveland: A Study in Courage, *by Allan Nevins (Dodd, Mead, 1932).*

was sent westward to help in organizing Union forces in Kentucky. He considered that this area was of crucial importance defensively, and that offensively "the Mississippi River will be a grand theater of war . . . I think it of more importance than Richmond"; but he soon found that raising troops in Kentucky was an even harder job than rallying them near Washington. The next few months proved the most exasperating period of his life. His immediate superior collapsed under the strain, leaving Sherman, who took over from him reluctantly, to deal with both the military and the political difficulties.

His outbursts of temper in trying to inject some discipline into the motley collection of volunteers had already led them to nickname him "Old Pills," and he now came into bitter conflict with the local politicians and press. He also had a clash with Secretary of War Simon Cameron, who came to Louisville on a short visit. Sherman, pointing out that he had only 20,000 men to cover a frontage of 300 miles, argued that at least 60,000 were needed for the immediate purpose, and 200,000 for an effective offensive down the Mississippi—a moderate estimate compared with the strength eventually expended. But the Secretary of War described it as an "insane" demand, and this careless phrase was exploited by Sherman's political and press critics, who now depicted him as a lunatic.

Such a blaring press campaign made his position impossible, so he suggested that it might be better if he were relieved of his command. His suggestion was promptly accepted, and he was transferred to a subordinate place under General Henry W. Halleck in the Department of the Missouri. But the stories about his insanity had preceded him, and he was looked at askance in many quarters, so that his own depression became acute. Relief came with the launching of the Union offensive in the West, which diverted the attention of the press to a fresh topic.

The offensive opened on January 19, 1862, when George H. Thomas broke the right end of the Confederate line by his victory at Mill Springs, Kentucky. It took on full momentum a few weeks later with the capture, by a spearhead force under Ulysses S. Grant, of Fort Henry on the Tennessee River and Fort Donelson on the Cumberland. In the next stage of the advance up the Tennessee, Sherman commanded a division under Grant, and his performance in the confused and seesaw Battle of Shiloh drew a special tribute from Grant to his "great judgment and skill on the management of his men." Halleck reported that Sherman had saved the situation and recommended that he be pro-

moted to the rank of major general, which was done.

The Union offensive subsequently fizzled out as a result of diverging efforts, sluggish movements, and Confederate raids on its railroad lines of supply. But the comradeship which linked Sherman and Grant from Shiloh on, and the intuitive teamwork they developed, bore good fruit in the 1863 campaign—after the too-cautious Halleck had been shifted to Washington as general in chief and Grant had taken his place in the West. Sherman, now given command of a corps, was Grant's right hand in the bold strategic maneuver that, after a series of failures, brought about the fall of Vicksburg on July 4, 1863, and thereby gained complete control of the Mississippi. The Confederacy was thus deprived permanently of reinforcements and supplies from the trans-Mississippi states—with effects more far-reaching than the repulse of Lee at Gettysburg, which took place at the same moment.

Grant's approach to Vicksburg had started in mid-April when Union gunboats and transports, loaded with supplies, ran the gantlet of the Confederate batteries under cover of night to establish a new base some thirty miles south of the fortress. Grant then filtered two of his three corps down there by a newly made road on the west bank of the Mississippi, and crossed to the east bank with little opposition, helped by a distraction which Sherman created above Vicksburg. When Sherman's corps rejoined him, bringing a large wagon train with fresh supplies, Grant cut loose from his new base and marched northeastward on May 7 to place his army astride Vicksburg's line of supply and reinforcement from the east and drive Confederate General John C. Pemberton and his army back into Vicksburg. Although the Confederate garrison of Vicksburg beat off his assaults, its isolation and growing starvation produced its surrender six weeks later.

There was no immediate strategic exploitation of the Vicksburg victory, and the next move was delayed by prolonged arguments in Washington as to where and how Grant's army should be employed. The arguments were settled fortuitously, and in the end fortunately, by the misfortune that General William S. Rosecrans' Army of the Cumberland suffered in Tennessee. Its southward advance in September met a heavy defeat at Chickamauga, and it became bottled up at Chattanooga. In this emergency Grant was given over-all command in the West, and Sherman succeeded to the command of his army. Grant moved to the rescue of Rosecrans and after a tough fight drove back the investing army. This victory opened the gateway into Georgia, the granary of the Confederacy, and thence into the eastern states as a whole. But in the following year, 1864, the Union came near to forfeiting the ultimate victory that appeared to be strategically assured. For the people of the North were growing weary under the prolonged strain of the struggle, and the peace party was gaining strength. The presidential election was due in November, and Lincoln was in danger of being ousted in favor of a President pledged to seek a compromise peace. He urgently needed to provide the people with clear evidence that there was good hope of early victory, and to this end he sent for Grant to take over the supreme command. Sherman was then appointed chief commander in the West; the "lunatic" now had 219,907 men, of whom about 100,000 were available for offensive operations in northern Georgia. For the coming campaign in the East, the main theatre, Grant chose the old direct overland approach southward from the Rappahannock River toward Richmond, counting on his greatly superior weight of numbers to smash Lee's army, or at least to wear it down by a "continuous hammering."

His own "will to conquer," however, did not bring success. He failed to smash Lee's army, while the strength of his own had withered in the fierce battles of the Wilderness and Cold Harbor. The only strategic advantage gained—that of having worked close to the rear of Richmond—looked like a stalemate. The northern people were discouraged, and at the end of the summer Lincoln doubted that he could be re-elected. Yet when the outlook seemed darkest, it suddenly lightened, and in the November elections Lincoln was returned to power. Sherman's capture of Atlanta in September was the saving factor.

There was deep mutual understanding between Grant and Sherman, but there was also a significant contrast in outlook. Grant's success as a commander had been largely due to the way he applied "horse sense" unfettered by the harness of military doctrine and custom, but he had no marked originality of con-

cept. Sherman was a man of vision, but started the war with the handicap of being too well versed in prevailing military theory and tactical manuals, and it was only when war experience helped to break this crust that his capacity for original thought had full play.

By 1864 the difference between the two men became apparent. While Grant's primary objective was the enemy's army, Sherman's was the seizure of strategic points. Atlanta, the base of the Confederate army opposing him in Georgia, was not only the junction of four important railways but also the source of vital supplies. As Sherman pointed out, it was "full of foundries, arsenals, and machine shops," as well as being of great importance psychologically as a symbol, and he held that "its capture would be the death knell of the Confederacy."

In the advance to Atlanta, Sherman's skill in maneuver was all the more notable because, by contrast to Grant in Virginia, he was tied to one railway line for his supplies. Moreover his starting point at Chattanooga was about 150 miles from his Nashville base and 330 miles from Louisville, the main source of supplies. That long line of supplies, lengthening as he advanced, was under threat everywhere from the raids of enemy cavalry and guerrillas. Yet, rather than commit his troops to a direct attack on an opponent well placed to block him, Sherman cut loose temporarily even from this supply line.

His ability to maneuver had been aided by the drastic way in which he cut down transport before starting. Each division and brigade was allotted only enough wagons to carry food and ammunition, and every man brought five days' rations on his person or horse. Apart from these supply trains, only one wagon and one ambulance was allowed to each regiment, with a pack mule for the mess kit and baggage of the officers of each company. Tents were forbidden, except for the sick and wounded and one for each headquarters as an office. Clerical work in the field was reduced to a minimum by the use of permanent offices in the rear for

Leslie's Weekly

November, 1864: Sherman burns Atlanta.

the transaction and transmission of all routine correspondence. This made possible a severe restriction of the size of the various headquarters staffs.

Sherman's own habit of living "rough" made his troops more ready to follow his example, while his lack of regard for outward appearance and the trappings of dignity strongly appealed to such pioneer types. So did his air of restless energy and constant alertness. At night he would often be seen prowling around the camp with his feet in old slippers, his legs covered only by a pair of red flannel drawers, his tall, spare body wrapped in a travel-worn dressing gown, with sometimes a short blue cape or cloak over all as a concession to convention. He was the lightest sleeper in his army, and by four o'clock in the morning liked to be up and about, thinking or listening—for that, he said, was "the best time to hear any movement at a distance." While his eccentricities endeared him to the troops, his alertness inspired their confidence, and "There's Uncle Billy. All's right," became a common saying.

More forgiving than most commanders where tactical errors occurred, knowing that the enemy's resistance and counteraction is the most incalculable factor in war, Sherman would rarely tolerate excuses for delays in the movement of supplies, believing that, by due foresight, preparation, and initiative, material obstacles could always be overcome. Those who obstructed or clung to the letter of regulations suffered sharply from his tongue. One officer who made difficulties was spurred to overcome them by the vehement retort, "If you don't have my army supplied, and keep it supplied, we'll eat your mules up, sir—eat your mules up." Later in the advance, when there was urgent need to replace a burnt railroad bridge and the chief engineer estimated that he would require four days for the task, Sherman is credited with the reply, "Sir, I give you forty-eight hours or a position in the front ranks."

When he had taken Atlanta, Sherman took a much bolder course, which carried greater strategic risks but diminished tactical risks. He felt sure that if he could march through Georgia and wreck its railway system, and then continue in the same way through South and North Carolina, the psychological impact of this strategic thrust into the heart of the South, coupled with the material effect of stopping the northward flow of supplies to Richmond and Lee's army, would produce the collapse of the Confederacy's resistance. So, ignoring Hood's army, which he had forced to evacuate Atlanta, he abandoned his own line of supply and set out on his famous "march to the sea" through Georgia—moving with the minimum of transport and living on the country while destroying its railways.

Starting from Atlanta in mid-November, he reached the outskirts of Savannah within four weeks and there reopened his communications, this time by sea. A discerning Confederate commander and historian, General E. P. Alexander, wrote that "the moral effect of this march . . . was greater than would have been the most decided victory."

At the beginning of February, 1865, Sherman moved northward through the Carolinas toward Lee's rear. By mid-March, after reaching North Carolina, he heard from Grant that Lee's army "is now demoralized and deserting very fast, both to us and to their homes." Yet Grant's own army was still immobilized in the trench lines round Petersburg and Richmond, where it had been brought to a halt the previous summer. It was not until the beginning of April that Grant resumed his advance. This now had a quick and dramatic success—retreating from Richmond, Lee's army was headed off and forced to surrender within a week.

Sherman's conduct of operations during the campaigns of 1864 and 1865 showed that the North had found a strategist who had diagnosed the causes of the prevalent paralysis and developed a remedy for it.

The increased facility of supply that came with the development of railroads had led commanders to build up increased numbers of troops at the railhead, without pausing to consider the hampering effect on their own power of maneuver. Thus the first result of the new means of strategic movement was, paradoxically, to reduce strategic mobility. The railroad fostered the expansion of armies—it could forward and feed many more than could operate effectively. It also tended to inflate their wants and demands, so that they became more closely tied to the railhead.

A further result was that their own strategic vulnerability increased because their sustenance and progress "hung on a thread"—the long stretch of rail line behind them, which could be all too easily cut by a small force maneuvering in such wide spaces. The Northern armies, accustomed to more plentiful rations, were more susceptible to paralysis than their opponents. That became increasingly evident in 1864, when, with growing strength, they pushed deeper into hostile territory. In the western theater the precarious situation of such rail-fed masses was exploited by the mobile raids of such brilliant Confederate cavalry leaders as Nathan Bedford Forrest and John Hunt Morgan.

Sherman grasped the problem and produced a solution—the only one then technically possible. The enemy had struck him through his rail communications; he would strike at theirs, while immunizing himself.

He saw that to regain and secure mobility he must free himself from dependence on a fixed line of supply. So he organized a force that was self-contained as to supplies, carrying the necessary minimum along with it and supplementing this by foraging from the countryside through which it passed. He then cut loose from his own railway.

Having shown in the march through Georgia how light an army could travel, Sherman now proved that it could move lighter still. Before starting northward through the Carolinas, he sought to convert his army "into a mobile machine willing and able to start at a moment's notice and to subsist on the scantiest of food." Although it was winter, officers as well as men were now made to bivouac in pairs under a strip of canvas stretched over sticks or boughs; all tents and camp furniture were discarded. Once again, as in his march on Atlanta, Sherman took a deceptive line between alternative objectives so that, time after time, his opponents could not concentrate their forces effectively to stop him.

Sherman's flexible organization of his army contributed almost as much as his variability of direction to his continuous progress. Moving on a wide and irregular front—with four, five, or six columns, each covered by a cloud of foragers—if one was blocked, others would be pushing on. The opposing forces became so jumpy that they repeatedly gave way to the psychological pressure and fell back before they felt any serious physical pressure. The mere shout, "We're Bill Sherman's raiders, you'd better git," sometimes sufficed to make opposing detachments retreat.

Sherman's strategy, and grand strategy, foreshadowed the aim that was pursued in the Allies' strategic bombing campaign of the Second World War. But that bombing offensive was too gradual in development to produce a quickly decisive effect, while it offered no such good opportunity for the opposing troops and people to escape from their leaders' grip by desertion and surrender—for it is not possible to surrender to an attacker who stays aloft in the sky. A closer parallel to, and fulfillment of, Sherman's strategy is to be found in the paralyzing and demoralizing shock effect, on the opposing armies and peoples simultaneously, of the blitzkriegs of 1939–41 carried out by the Germans, who combined deep thrusting armored forces with air attack.

Since General Heinz Guderian, the creator and leader of the panzer forces, has stated that he derived this new technique from my writings, it may be of historical interest to mention that the concept developed in my mind partly in studying the course and effect of Sherman's operations.

This was the first war between modern democracies,

UNCLE BILLY CHANGED HIS MIND

Mr. Lincoln had just been installed, and the newspapers were filled with rumors of every kind indicative of war; the chief act of interest was that Major Robert Anderson had taken by night into Fort Sumter all the troops garrisoning Charleston Harbor, and that he was determined to defend it against the demands of the State of South Carolina and of the Confederate States. I must have reached Washington about the 10th of March. I found my brother there, just appointed Senator, in place of Mr. Chase, who was in the cabinet, and I have no doubt my opinions, thoughts, and feelings, wrought up by the events in Louisiana, seemed to him gloomy and extravagant. About Washington I saw but few signs of preparation, though the Southern Senators and Representatives were daily sounding their threats on the floors of Congress, and were publicly withdrawing to join the Confederate Congress at Montgomery. Even in the War Department and about the public offices there was open, unconcealed talk, amounting to high-treason.

One day, John Sherman took me with him to see Mr. Lincoln. He walked into the room where the secretary to the President now sits, we found the room full of people, and Mr. Lincoln sat at the end of the table, talking with three or four gentlemen, who soon left. John walked up, shook hands, and took a chair near him, holding in his hand some papers referring to minor appointments in the State of Ohio, which formed the subject of conversation. Mr. Lincoln took the papers, said he would refer them to the proper heads of departments, and would be glad to make the appointments asked for, if not already promised. John then turned to me, and said, "Mr. President, this is my brother, Colonel Sherman, who is just up from Louisiana, he may give you some information you want." "Ah" said Mr. Lincoln, "how are they getting along down there?" I said, "They think they are getting along swimmingly—they are preparing for war." "Oh, well!" said he, "I guess we'll manage to keep house." I was silenced, said no more to him, and we soon left. I was sadly disappointed, and remember that I broke out on John, d—ning the politicians generally, saying, "You have got things in a hell of a fix, and you may get them out as you best can," adding that the country was sleeping on a volcano that might burst forth at any minute, but that I was going to St. Louis to take care of my family, and would have no more to do with it.

Memoirs of General W. T. Sherman, *Charles L. Webster & Co., New York, 1892*

and Sherman saw clearly that the resisting power of a democracy depends even more on the strength of the people's will than on the strength of its armies. His unchecked march through the heart of the South, destroying its resources, was the most effective way to create and spread a sense of helplessness that would undermine the will to continue the war.

The havoc that his march produced in the Deep South left a legacy of bitterness in later years—more than in the immediate postwar years. That has recoiled on Sherman's historical reputation. But it is questionable whether that bitterness or the impoverishment of the South would have been prolonged, or grave, if the peace settlement had not been dominated by the vindictiveness of the northern extremists who gained the upper hand after Lincoln's assassination.

For Sherman himself bore in mind the need of moderation in making peace. That was shown in the generous terms of the agreement he drafted for the surrender of Johnston's army—an offer for which he was violently denounced by the government in Washington. Moreover, he persistently pressed the importance, for the future of the forcibly reunited nation, of reconciling the conquered section by good treatment and help toward its recovery. His vision extended beyond the horizon of war to the peace that would follow.

B. H. Liddell Hart, an internationally recognized authority on military tactics and strategy, and especially on mechanized warfare, retired from the British Army in 1927.

For further reading: Captain Liddell Hart's Sherman *(Praeger, 1958), and* Sherman, Fighting Prophet, *by Lloyd Lewis (Harcourt, Brace, 1958).*

Never Alone At Last CONTINUED FROM PAGE 31

This sketch from an 1830 broadside advertised one of Chang and Eng's first tours.

his Adelaide. Eng had twelve by his Sarah Ann. As family men, they were much respected in the Carolina hills. Their descendants are today well-regarded citizens of North Carolina; one great-great-grandson, a banker, still carries the friendly nickname "Chink." (The roster of their scions has also included a president of the Union Pacific Railroad and a major general in the U.S. Air Force.)

There are no records upon which to base speculation about the conjugal relations of Chang, Eng, Adelaide, and Sarah Ann. Obviously their relationship was always a triangle if not a foursome. Under such circumstances it is not too hard to understand the early report that "their collateral domestic life was unhappy." The sister-wives quarreled, so that the brother-husbands were forced to maintain separate establishments. They made a firm pact that they would spend three days in one house and three days in the other. Perhaps on the seventh day they rested.

That brief "last" period of exhibition in 1853 did not suffice. Chang and Eng suffered financially after the Civil War, particularly from the loss of their slaves. A shy but enterprising young Confederate veteran, Major Henry A. London, on returning home after Lee's surrender, became interested in helping the twins as a means of helping himself in desperate times. Recently his daughter recalled:

After the War Between the States my father, who was 18 years old, and his brother-in-law, Mr. Zimmerman, went to the Siamese twins in Mt. Airy to see if they would be interested in making some money (as everyone in the South was broke) and be exhibited again in the North. They were delighted over the idea, so Father and Mr. Zimmerman became the advance press agents, going to various organizations and displaying the pictures of the Siamese twins, etc. When they came to Baltimore and the fashionable resort of Cape May, Mr. Zimmerman would stay in his room as he was so afraid he would be seen by some of his friends. They did this for a season and all made some much needed money.

Not satisfied with the proceeds of Major London's efforts, Chang and Eng set out for Europe again, this time under the more expert direction of P. T. Barnum. While returning from Liverpool to America in 1870, Chang had a paralytic stroke during one of his increasingly frequent alcoholic debauches. As this involved his left arm and leg, Eng henceforth carried much of Chang's weight.

Back on their plantations in North Carolina, on

Monday, January 12, 1874, Chang developed a "dry cough with scanty, frothy sputum." He complained, too, of a pain in his chest. Dr. Hollingsworth directed that he not venture out. Nevertheless, on Thursday, the usual day to move to Eng's house, he honored the agreement, and they made the trip in an open buggy in very cold weather. Eng remained in excellent health throughout Chang's illness. On Friday Chang felt better but that night he "had such severe pain in the chest, and so much distress he thought he would die."

The twins were alone in a room with a young son of Eng's. Sometime in the course of the night they got up and sat by the fire. Eng wanted to retire but Chang insisted upon sitting up, as his "breathing was so bad that it would kill me to lie down." Finally about one o'clock they went to bed; after an hour or so the family heard someone call but no one went to them.

Later Eng awakened and asked his son, "How is your Uncle Chang?"

The boy said, "Uncle Chang is cold—Uncle Chang is dead."

When Eng's wife entered the room, he began crying out to her: "My last hour is come . . . I am dying."

He did not speak of his brother's death.

"He rubbed his upper extremities," the old medical records say, "and raised them restlessly, and complained of a choking sensation. The only notice he took of Chang was to move nearer to him. Eng's last words were, 'May the Lord have mercy upon my soul.'"

Dr. Hollingsworth did not reach the house until both twins were dead. Though the family were averse to an autopsy, he obtained consent to put the bodies in a position to be preserved until he could obtain an expert to perform one. The bodies were cooled and placed in a coffin that was put in a wooden box enclosed in tin; this was imbedded in charcoal in the dry cellar of Eng's home. William Augustus Reich, the local tinsmith, in a letter (probably to his sister) written from Mt. Airy on January 19, 1874, told about the unusual coffin:

Dear Darling J

I write you a few lines this morning. I expect you heard the Siamese twins are dead. I got an order late Saturday evening for a large tin coffin. I made it. I worked nearly all night, finished it about noon yesterday. Cut out yesterday afternoon and soldered them up. It was a sight the people that was there. It was a long time before I could get my foot in at the door, so crowded. It was like a camp meeting so many people horses and carriages. It was most night before I got through soldering them up. They are not going to bury them but keep them in the house. I expect they are afraid somebody would steal them. The Siamese twins is the greatest human curiosity in the world and who ever thought I would be the man to solder them up. I had to cut into 34 big sheets of tin to make the coffin. I have a notion to charge

$20 do you think that would be about right? Their death was sudden and unexpected on Friday night late. . . . All the doctors went out Saturday morning prepared to cut them apart, but they were both dead when they got there. I heard somebody say that Chang had always been accustomed to liquor, but had not used any for a few days and perhaps caused a reaction. . . . They were both real business men and have large families. . . . The Siamese twins were nicely dressed in black with slippers on. I helped lift them in their coffin it was a strange sight. I must close with our best love I remain

Affectionately

Augustus

It was a sight to see the people that came to my house to see me make this coffin. It was the greatest job I ever done. I send you a drop of solder that dropped on the coffin as I was soldering them up yesterday.

Shortly after the death of the twins, Dr. William Pancoast, of a family of famous Philadelphia physicians, requested the mayor of Philadelphia to telegraph the mayor of Greensboro, North Carolina, seeking permission for an autopsy. The mayor of Greensboro replied that he had no knowledge or power in the matter. A week after the death, Dr. Hollingsworth met in Philadelphia with Dr. Pancoast and Professor Samuel D. Gross, of Jefferson Medical College, and a letter was dispatched to the widows of Chang and Eng proposing that Dr. Pancoast come to embalm and examine the bodies. A commission consisting of Dr. Pancoast and Dr. Harrison Allen, famous anatomist of the University of Pennsylvania, with a Dr. Andrews as companion and aide, arrived in Mt. Airy on January 31, two weeks after the twins' death.

At a conference with the widows, it was agreed that, as a consideration for embalming the bodies, permission would be granted to exhume and to examine the structure between them, provided that no incision be made that would impair the external surface of the band. Later a written agreement allowed the bodies to be taken to Philadelphia, if kept safe in a fireproof building.

Great and curious crowds of Carolinians gathered to help the commission exhume the bodies, which were carried to a large chamber for photographs and autopsy. The room was then cleared of all except the commission. The bodies were found well preserved, and embalming was begun. It was found that the aortas of both twins were marked by fatty degeneration—Chang's so much so that the chloride of zinc used as an embalming agent had to be injected in the lower part of the abdomen rather than downward through the aorta. It was soon decided that a better autopsy could be done in Philadelphia. Back the bodies went into the coffin and into Gus Reich's tin masterpiece and into an express car, and thence to the College of Physicians and Surgeons in Philadelphia. There they were placed under the care of the commission in the Mutter Museum and were closely locked and guarded.

At a well-attended meeting of the College on February 18, the commission exhibited the bodies and demonstrated the findings. These indicated that the band of union connected the twins at the abdominal segment of the breastbone. It contained peritoneal pouches and an extension of liver substance from each abdomen. Vascular connections were sparse but colored plaster material injected into the portal circulation of Chang was found to flow into Eng's portal vessels as far down as the lower abdominal cavity. The limitations imposed by the widows on the extent of the autopsy left certain anatomical features unclear. It was found that the lower pointed ends of the hearts "present toward each other." The bladder of Chang, who died first, was found contracted and empty, while Eng's was markedly distended with urine.

In discussions of his findings before the College, Dr. Pancoast made no statement as to the cause of Chang's death but speculated about Eng's: "Probably the valves of his heart were in a disorganized condition, and probably also the shock [of Chang's death] upon that weakened organ caused death."

Dr. Harrison Allen said,

In my opinion, Chang died of a cerebral clot. From inquiry at his home, I was led to believe that the lung symptoms were not due to pneumonia; indeed, were not severe enough to have been so caused. The suddenness of the death, the general atheroma [fatty inner degeneration] of the arteries, and the fact that there has been previously an attack of cerebral paralysis, all indicated that the death was of cerebral origin. Eng probably died of fright as the distended bladder seemed to point to a profound emotional disturbance of the nervous system, the mind remaining clear until stupor came on,—a stupor which was probably syncopal [i.e., due to cerebral anemia]!

A modern medical man, Dr. Worth B. Daniels of Washington, D.C., has also speculated upon the cause of death. In a paper delivered before the American Clinical and Climatological Association, of which he is president, Dr. Daniels began by reviewing the known facts. Chang had severe atherosclerosis and had suffered a cerebral thrombosis. Five days before his death he developed a cough productive of frothy sputum and some chest pain. Chang's death was so quiet it did not awaken Eng. This would indicate, Dr. Daniels thought, that Chang's death was not due purely to the pulmonary edema.

"It was," he said, using a succession of medical terms, "probably sudden as might occur with an abnormal rhythm. It appears to me that the diagnoses in Chang's case were: (1) Xiphopagic twin. (2) Generalized atherosclerosis. (3) Coronary atherosclerosis. (4) Myocardial infarction. (5) Congestive heart failure with pulmonary edema. (6) Arrhythmia, probably ventricular fibrillation."

Then he added: "In Eng's case, I fully agree with Dr. Harrison Allen. Eng died of fright. If you doubt this try being joined to a dead, xiphopagic twin!"

Could the twins have been separated safely? Considering the medical conditions of the time, probably not. Efforts at separation prior to the introduction of anaesthesia and aseptic surgical techniques were fraught with great danger. Most such attempts resulted in the deaths of both twins. Frequently, even now, the connecting structures are so vital to the survival of both individuals that separation is still hazardous. This is particularly true when the union involves the heads and brain or brain coatings and the spine or the covering of the spinal cords.

But it seems probable that Chang and Eng—or other twins joined in the same way—could be readily separated by a skilled surgeon today. The only vital structure observed in their case, the extension of the liver, could be divided and sutured and the operative wound closed, as is done with an abdominal hernia. But during the lifetime of the brothers from Siam, entry into the abdominal cavity frequently produced peritonitis and death.

Following the autopsy in Philadelphia, the twins were repacked in their tin container and shipped back to North Carolina. Soon they would be forgotten as men who had inescapably lived and loved and died together. They had become just two southerners who, leaving behind them numerous American progeny, were sleeping in their tin coffin in the graveyard of a country Baptist church in North Carolina. But the name by which they were called, in screaming banners above the gates of museums of marvels in America and Europe, may remain forever as the description of all xiphopagic twins, those whom God hath, quite literally, joined together. Chang and Eng, who were inseparable when they lived, remain inseparable in recollection forever.

A native of North Carolina and one of America's eminent journalists, Jonathan Worth Daniels is the editor of the Raleigh News and Observer. *Toward the end of World War II he served as administrative assistant to President Franklin D. Roosevelt. He is the author of many books, the most recent of which is* The Devil's Backbone, *a history of the Natchez Trace, published by McGraw-Hill.*

READING, WRITING, AND HISTORY

By BRUCE CATTON

Objective Viewpoint

Speaking to an audience in Richmond early in January, 1863, Jefferson Davis undertook to remind all southerners of the oppressive weight which a Northern conquest would inevitably bring to them. The weight was being felt, as he spoke, within much less than one hundred miles of the Confederate capital, and President Davis was eloquent about it.

"The Northern portion of Virginia," he remarked, "has been ruthlessly desolated—the people not only deprived of the means of subsistence, but their household property destroyed and every indignity which the base imagination of a merciless foe could suggest inflicted without regard to age, sex or condition."

That Mr. Davis had genuine evils to complain about is undeniable. Northern Virginia had known the harsh rule of General John Pope, and it had had even rougher treatment from undisciplined cavalrymen and straggling foot soldiers who overran towns and plantation houses with a casual rowdiness that was the essence of unstudied and unprovoked brutality. Yet the present generation, to its sorrow, has learned things about oppression which the generation of the 1860's did not know. The armies of Germany and Russia have shown the hideous things that can happen when an invader really casts aside restraint and sets out to break a conquered people. The words, "every indignity which the base imagination of a merciless foe could suggest," have a meaning now which President Davis, General Pope, and the wayward Union soldier could not possibly

have imagined. By this time we have known foes who were genuinely and literally merciless and whose imaginations could descend to a depth of baseness not conceivable to the innocence of a century ago.

President Davis' indignation, in short, was justified, but his language meant a great deal less in 1863 than it would mean today. We know now how far "the base imagination of a merciless foe" can go, and if we forget, there are plenty of people in places like Poland and the Ukraine who could refresh our memories. Seen in the light of things that happened overseas in the years after 1940, the American Civil War calls for a milder commentary than once seemed justified. It brought an abundance of cruelty and baseness upon the land, but they were not the cruelty and baseness which our generation has had to know about. Ben Butler, for example, was about as malodorous a governor of occupied territory as the Civil War produced, but he seems positively benign by comparison with military governors recently seen in Europe.

These meditations arise from a reading of Mr. Edmund Wilson's newest book, *Patriotic Gore*, which is a discussion, by a most eminent literary critic, of the literature of the Civil War. (Not the literature *about* the war; Mr. Wilson concerns himself with material written by men and women who were actually in it, from Abraham Lincoln and U. S. Grant to Mary Chesnut and John W. De Forest.) In his introduction to this thoughtful and useful work Mr. Wilson remarks that he feels "under some obligation to explain to the reader in advance the general point of view which gives shape to my picture of the war."

The war reminds him, to begin with, of one voracious sea slug swallowing another; a power struggle, pure and simple, which impels him to try "to remove the whole subject from the plane of morality and to give an objective account of the expansion of the United States." Like Bismarck and Lenin, Abraham Lincoln was engaged in unifying a great power; like them he became an uncompromising dictator; and "each was succeeded by agencies which continued to exercise this power and to manipulate the peoples he had been unifying in a stupid, despotic and unscrupulous fashion, so that all the bad potentialities of the policies he had initiated were realized, after his removal, in the most undesirable way."

Thus, after the war, the Radical Republicans in Washington "added every form of insult and injury to the bitterness of the Confederate failure." "We Americans have not yet had to suffer from the worst of the calamities that have followed on the dictatorships in Germany and Russia, but we have been going for a long time now quite steadily in the same direction." This leads Mr. Wilson to ask: "In what way, for example, was the fate of Hungary, at the time of its recent rebellion, any worse than the fate of the South at the end of the Civil War?"

Now this, really, is the language of the 1860's all over again, unmodified by afterknowledge. Did the Republican regime in Washington, after Lincoln's death, really inflict upon the South "every form of insult and injury"—*every* form, as the business would be understood nowadays? There were no executions and there were no concentration camps or proscription lists or confiscation of estates. Within very little more than ten years the army of occupation was withdrawn, southerners ruled their own lives as they saw fit, and former Confederate generals took their seats in the Senate and the House of Representatives. The fate of Hungary was no worse than this?

It is of course perfectly true that the South remembers the Civil War with deep emotions; true also that the federal government's recent attempt to enforce integration in schools has met with a great deal of

---

Patriotic Gore, by Edmund Wilson. Oxford University Press. 816 pp. $8.50.

---

resistance. But what on earth is one to make of this assertion?—"The truth is that the South since the Civil War, in relation to the Washington government, has been in a state of mind that has fluctuated between that of Hungary and that of the Ukraine in relation to the government of Moscow."

What is being talked about in this introduction is not literature but history, and it is worthwhile to see what kind of history is being expounded. It is the story, apparently, of one sea slug swallowing another. . . . We entered World War I, says Mr. Wilson, because of British propaganda, although "we might well by abstaining have shortened the war and left Europe less shattered and more stable." We were "gradually and furtively" brought into the Second World War by Mr. Roosevelt, who appears to have maneuvered the Japanese into bombing Pearl Harbor—in about the same way, apparently, that Mr. Lincoln maneuvered the Confederacy into firing on Fort Sumter. Now we are in a cold war, and our problem is that we persist in attaching abstract values to it and refuse to recognize the whole tragic affair as a business of sea slugs.

As noted above, Mr. Wilson begins by promising to explain his general point of view and to give an objective account of the regrettable unpleasantness of the 1860's. The point of view is clearly set forth, but the "objectivity" is that of The Debunker: the most impassioned and pontifical objectivity you are likely to meet in a long, long time.

Negro's Viewpoint

For relief, turn to another treatment. In *Lincoln and the Negro*, Mr. Benjamin Quarles discusses one poignant aspect of the Civil War which cannot easily be reduced to terms of sea slugs: the business of the Negroes who lived just below the ladder's bottom rung when the war began and who found in the war, in spite of all the odds, a chance to start climbing.

Mr. Quarles has a point of view of his own, the substance of which apparently is that what people think about an action taken—what they feel deep in their hearts, what they respond to with their blood and muscles and their dreams—may in the end mean even more than the action itself; may in fact transfigure the action and make it contain more than the actor himself originally meant. It may, finally, confound the mathematics of the pundit who adds two and two together and finds that the answer cannot possibly be anything greater than a meager four.

He concerns himself here, chiefly, with the Emancipation Proclamation.

Any way you look at it, here was a very odd document. It represented the very least that a wartime President (concerned, somehow, that the war which was costing so many lives ought to be a little bit more than a matter of one slug swallowing another) could do about the terrible issue of human slavery. It was a timid pronunciamento, an attempt to carry water on both shoulders, a politician's halfhearted stab at seeming to do something without actually doing it. It ordained that slaves would be free in precisely those areas where the Federal government lacked power to enforce its edict; where the Federal government was in full control, with marshals and courts and great ranks of soldiers to make the writ good, slavery was left untouched. It even permitted the states which had seceded to retain their slaves if they would just come back into the Union in three months' time. Altogether, as Mr. Quarles points out, it "sounded like a cross between a military directive and a lawyer's brief." It was an instrument of developing war policy, nothing more or less, coldly conceived and attaining eloquence only because its central paragraph ended with the words "forever free." It would mean as much, or as little, as the government tried to make it mean.

A fraud, then, offering nothing of consequence to a luckless pawn? (To Mr. Wilson, the contemplated destruction of slavery was "the rabble-rousing moral issue which is necessary in every modern war to make the conflict appear as a melodrama.") It might have gone that way—except that the Negroes themselves, who after all had the most direct stake in the matter, believed it. Believing it, they turned the Emancipation Proclamation into one of the most powerful and significant utterances any American President has ever made.

Mr. Quarles emphasizes that the Negroes were not being deceived. They knew that the edict of September 22, 1862, was "little more than the declaration of an intention," and that there was "nothing in custom or in law" that could force the President to follow it up. But they believed in it, and believed in it so fervently that—as Mr. Quarles puts it—the Proclamation "changed the whole tone and character of the war." They saw it before Lincoln himself did, and their belief had much to do with the fact that it quickly took on "the evocative power reserved only for the half-dozen great charter expressions of human liberty in the entire Western tradition."

Not the least of the people on whom this faith had its full effect was Lincoln himself. In the long weeks between his issuance of the preliminary Proclamation, just after the Battle of Antietam, and the final proclamation in January, 1863, Lincoln appears to have wavered. He was not quite sure, even then, or for that matter a good deal later. On July 31, 1863, after Gettysburg and Vicksburg had underlined his final authority, he wrote, broodingly: "I think I shall not retract or repudiate it," quite as if the matter were still up for final decision. But he stayed with it, partly because the people in bondage had taken him at his word.

How could he do otherwise? Mr. Quarles recites the familiar story about the gang of ex-slaves who were working for the quartermaster corps at a Federal army outpost in South Carolina while the war was still on. They were talking about Lincoln and what he had done and might yet do, and one white-haired patriarch interrupted them sternly by saying: "What do you know 'bout Massa Linkum? Massa Linkum be ebrewhere. He walk de earth like de Lord." No man can swim against that sort of current. The doubt and hesitation which are only partly hidden beneath the long, lawyerlike phrases of the Proclamation at last fell away, and Lincoln finally confessed that his issuance of this document "was the one thing that would make people remember that he had lived."

The thing of course had immediate practical effects. For one point, it got Negroes into the United States Army, which automatically made slavery a dead duck forever after. (You do not, after all, return to slavery—or even, permanently, to second-class citizenship—a man who has worn his country's uniform and endured battle for it.) For another, it gave the Negro the feeling that he had a stake in America and in all that America might mean. "As the war moved toward its close," says Mr. Quarles, "the Negro's sense of identity with the land of his birth grew deeper, nourished anew by its source—Abraham Lincoln."

This takes us a certain distance away from the resolute conviction that the Civil War meant nothing more than a power struggle between two greedy imperialisms. It *was* that, to be sure, and it is easy enough to recite the manifold uglinesses that it brought in its train. But although Mr. Wilson can point out that

---

Lincoln and the Negro, by Benjamin Quarles. Oxford University Press. 275 pp. $6.50.

---

when the federal government uses troops to get Negro children into schools, southerners "remember the burning of Atlanta, the wrecking by Northern troops of Southern homes, the disfranchisement of the governing classes and the premature enfranchisement of the Negroes," it still remains to be asked: What do the Negroes remember? Let Mr. Quarles answer:

"Because freedom is a deep river, Negroes would prefer to cross over in a calm time. But cross over they must, being Americans. And the Negroes of the Civil War years and after could find strength for the struggle by reflecting upon the life of a man who, on the threshold of his career, had said that this nation could not endure half slave and half free; a man who, at the midpoint of his presidency, had called upon his generation to highly resolve that America should have a new birth of freedom; and a man who, as the unseen shadows gathered around him, had exhorted his countrymen to strive on to finish the great work they were in."

Dream on, H. M. Small

There are many kinds of inventors. One is the heralded, or no-one-is-laughing-at-them-any-longer, variety, like Edison, Elias Howe, and the Wright Brothers. Then there are the heralded-for-something-else inventors, like Mark Twain, who devised a new kind of scrapbook, or Lillian Russell, who patented an improved trunk. (Her own scarcely needed any improvement.) But there is, alas, a sad, forgotten group, the inventors of useful and clever devices that never quite catch on. Some of the splendid ideas of these unsung geniuses are shown here in patent drawings picked out from a recent booklet on patents published by E. I. du Pont de Nemours & Company, where they know a good deal about the subject.

Consider the brilliant notion, at top, of H. M. Small; if the railroads cared, it would still be a good idea, as any tired commuter knows. Or Joseph Fallek's grapefruit shield; because no one listened, this mischievous fruit is still taking its annual toll at the national breakfast table. Nor is it too late to this very day for the President of the United States to snap up one of Clark's rocking-chair churns. It would not only relieve executive tensions, it would also help out around the White House.

1. *The Commuter's Friend, a hammock to rest the legs, was patented by H. M. Small in 1889.*

2. *The Rocking Churn sprang from the brain of one A. Clark, of East Corinth, Me., in 1913.*

3. *Not a space suit but, quite literally, a watery bathrobe was J. F. King's 1913 device.*

4. *A. L. McMurtry's Soap-Bubble Hat (1912). It might seem drab in today's Easter Parade.*

5. *Why spray your spouse when you could use Joseph Fallek's grapefruit shield (1928)?*

6. *If tipping one's hat without removing the hands from the pockets is good manners, this device is a forgotten landmark of etiquette.*

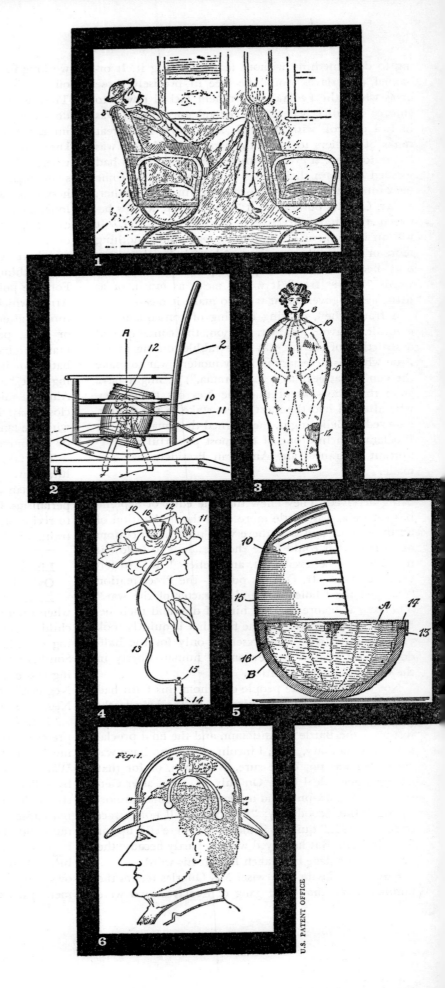